Advanced Crochet Projects For Adults

15 Advanced Crochet Patterns Book With Step-by-Step Instructions & Illustrations for Advanced Crocheters From Amigurumi to Afghan Blankets & Many More

Nancy Gordon

© **Copyright 2023 by Nancy Gordon - All rights reserved.**

The content contained within this book may not be reproduced, duplicated, or transmitted without direct written permission from the author or the publisher.

Under no circumstances will any blame or legal responsibility be held against the publisher, or author, for any damages, reparation, or monetary loss due to the information contained within this book, either directly or indirectly.

Legal Notice:

This book is copyright protected. It is only for personal use. You cannot amend, distribute, sell, use, quote, or paraphrase any part, or the content within this book, without the consent of the author or publisher.

Disclaimer Notice:

Please note the information contained within this document is for educational and entertainment purposes only. All effort has been executed to present accurate, up-to-date, reliable, complete information. No warranties of any kind are declared or implied.

Readers acknowledge that the author is not engaged in the rendering of legal, financial, medical, or professional advice. The content within this book has been derived from various sources. Please consult a licensed professional before attempting any techniques outlined in this book.

By reading this document, the reader agrees that under no circumstances is the author responsible for any losses, direct or indirect, that are incurred as a result of the use of the information contained within this document, including, but not limited to, errors, omissions, or inaccuracies.

Table of Contents

Introduction v

Chapter 1: Glossary.. 7

    Yarn Hooks Conversion Chart 11
    Steel Hooks Conversion Chart 14

Chapter 2: Patterns 17

    1. A Granny Square With a Difference................ 17
    2. A Snowflake Story 27
    3. Diamonds Are Forever 32
    4. A Tunisian Cowl 37
    5. Celtic Stitch Blanket 42
    6. Cables to Keep You Warm 46
    7. An Elegant Poncho With Heart Detail............50
    8. Bruges Lace Border..62
    9. A Classic Capelet in Broomstick Lace............ 68
    10. Tapestry Crochet Afghan Square 74
    11. A Flowing Butterfly Cardigan 79
    12. A Shawl in Contrasting Stripes for Colder Weather..99
    13. Wrap Yourself in Lattice Lace 106
    14. Amigurumi Octopus 112
    15. Poinsettias for the Holidays 118

Conclusion 124

    Review Request... 125

References 127

Introduction

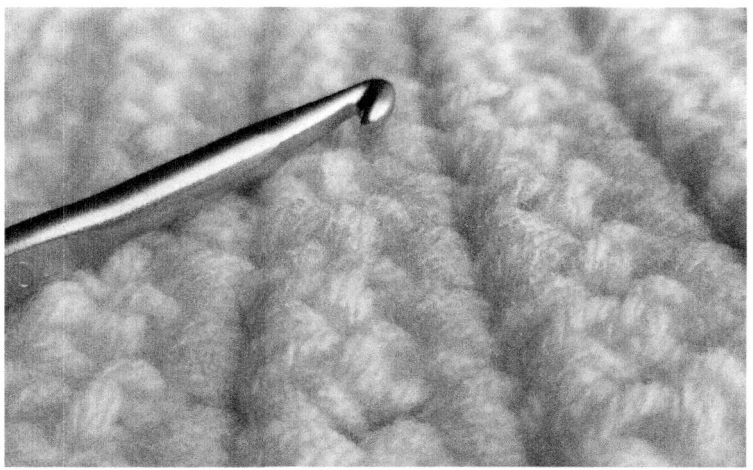

A beautiful crochet stitch.

"Crochet is an accessible art that comes with a license to be prolific". (Toukou, 2014).

When you are crocheting, do people look at you like you're a magician? You know, you waggle a stick around, mumble to yourself, and something new is born while no one knows what you're doing!

On a serious note, crochet aficionados know this craft to be one of the most rewarding and relaxing activities possible.

In this ebook, you will find several patterns for the more advanced crocheter. While a glossary of terms and abbreviations is provided in the next chapter, and you will find abbreviations and explanations of special stitches in every pattern, there are no explanations of beginner-level techniques.

Enjoy making these projects!

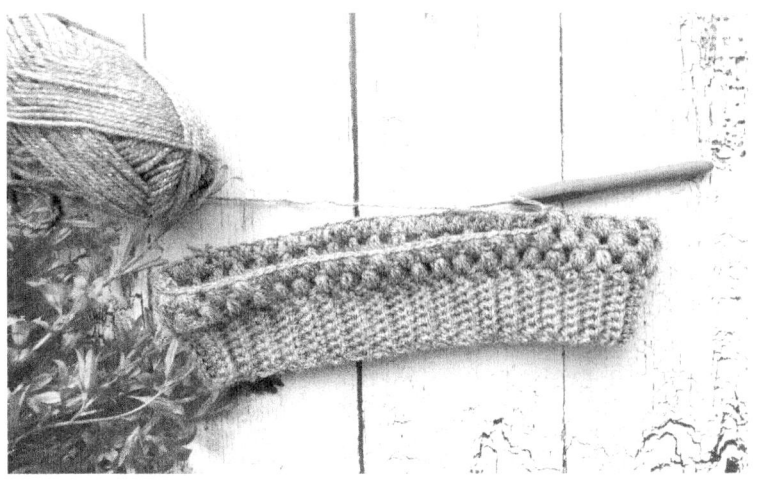

The start of another exciting crochet project.

Chapter 1: Glossary

Crochet and warm blankets go hand in hand.

The glossary with some of the commonly used abbreviations in this ebook is in the beginning of the ebook for ease of reference. It is taken from a master list of accepted abbreviations published by the US Craft Yarn Council (n.d.-a).

Both the yarn hook and steel hook size conversion tables are also included (Craft Yarn Council, n.d.-b).

Abbreviation	Description
alt	alternate
approx	approximately
beg	begin/beginning
bet	between
BL or BLO	back loop or back loop only
BP	back post
CC	contrasting color
ch	chain stitch
ch-	refer to chain or space previously made, e.g. ch-1 space
ch-sp	chain space
CL	cluster
cont	continue
dc	double crochet
dc2tog	double crochet 2 stitches together
dec	decrease
FL or FLO	front loop or front loop only
foll	following
FP	front post

Abbreviation	Description
inc	increase
lp	loop
MC	main color
pat/patt	pattern
pm	place marker
prev	previous
rem	remaining
rep	repeat
rnd	round
RS	right side
sc	single crochet
sk	skip
sl st	slip stitch
sp	space
st/s	stitch/es
TBL	through back loop
tch or t-ch	turning chain
tog	together
tc	treble/triple crochet

Abbreviation	Description
WS	wrong side
yo	yarn over
yoh	yarn over hook

Yarn Hooks Conversion Chart

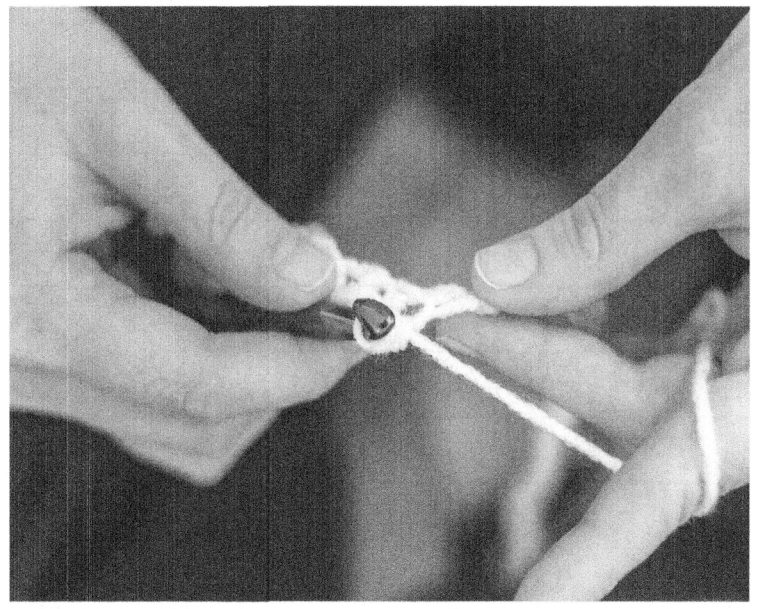

Colorful crochet hooks make the craft even more enjoyable.

US	Metric	Old UK/ Canada
-	2 mm	14
B-1	2.25 mm	13
-	2.5 mm	12
C-2	2.75 mm	-
-	3 mm	11

US	Metric	Old UK/ Canada
D-3	3.25 mm	10
E-4	3.5 mm	9
F-5	3.75 mm	-
G-6	4 mm	8
7	4.5 mm	7
H-8	5 mm	6
I-9	5.5 mm	5
J-10	6 mm	4
K-10.5	6.5 mm	3
-	7 mm	2
L-11	8 mm	0
M/N-13	9 mm	00
N/P-15	10 mm	000
P-16	11.5 mm	
-	12 mm	
P/Q	15 mm	
Q	15.75 mm	
Q	16 mm	
S	19 mm	

US	Metric	Old UK/ Canada
T/U/X	25 mm	
T/X	30 mm	

Steel Hooks Conversion Chart

Crochet hooks with wooden handles.

US	Metric
00	3.5 mm
0	3.25 mm
1	2.75 mm
00	2.7 mm
0	2.55 mm
1	2.35 mm
2	2.25 mm

US	Metric
2	2.2 mm
3	2.1 mm
4	2 mm
5	1.9 mm
6	1.8 mm
4/0	1.75 mm
5	1.7 mm
7	1.65 mm
6	1.6 mm
8/7/2	1.5 mm
9/8	1.4 mm
10	1.3 mm
9/4	1.25 mm
10	1.15 mm
11	1.1 mm
11	1.05 mm
12/6	1 mm
13	0.95 mm
14/8	0.90 mm

US	Metric
13	0.85 mm
14/10	0.75 mm
12	0.6 mm

Chapter 2: Patterns

"I find your lack of yarn disturbing."—Unknown

In this chapter, you will find a tempting collection of patterns sourced from various designers and in a variety of styles that will make you remedy any lack of yarn immediately.

1. A Granny Square With a Difference

This pattern uses monochrome wool with exquisite detail that offers surprises in every round (Holloway, 2018).

Supplies needed:

- 250-275 yards of #4 worsted weight yarn
- Crochet hook, H-8 (5 mm)
- A yarn sewing needle
- Scissors
- Blocking board (optional)

Abbreviations:

- ch = chain
- sk = skip
- st/s = stitch/es
- sl st = slip stitch
- sc = single crochet
- hdc = half double crochet
- dc = double crochet
- tr = treble crochet
- 2tr cluster = treble crochet 2 together in same st
- tr2tog = treble crochet 2 together (worked over top of the 2tr clusters, with one leg on each side of the cluster.)
- BPsc = back post single crochet
- BPhdc = back post half double crochet
- BPdc = back post double crochet
- FPsc = front post single crochet
- FPdc = front post double crochet
- FPtr = front post treble crochet

- BLO = back loop only
- sp/s = space/s

Gauge: A little over 3¼-inch across after round 6.

Specifics:

Picot sc = Insert hook, yo, pull up a loop, [yo, draw through 1 loop] 3 times to make a ch 3, then yo, and draw through the last loop on the hook.

3dc cluster = dc3tog in the same stitch.

Small puff st = yo, pull up a loop 3 times in the same st, yo, pull through 6 loops, yo, pull through final 2 loops.

Puff st = yo, pull up a loop 4 times in the same st, yo, pull through 8 loops, yo, pull through final 2 loops.

The final measurement of the square is 12 inches x 12 inches.

The square will not always lay flat while you are working on it but it will flatten out in the end. Any remaining issues can be fixed with some blocking.

Pattern:

Start: Magic circle.

Round 1: 6 sc in magic circle, join with sl st to first sc. (6 sc)

Round 2: Ch 1, working in BLO, 2 sc in each st around, join with sl st to first st. (12 sc)

Round 3: Ch 1, *small puff st, ch 1, move to next st; repeat from * around, join with sl st to first small puff. (12 small puffs, 12 ch)

Round 4: Ch 1, picot sc in first st, sc in next st * picot sc in next st, sc in next st; repeat from * around, join with sl st to first picot sc. (12 picot sc, 12 sc)

Round 5: Ch 1, sc in first st, 2 sc in next st *sc in next st, 2 sc in next st; repeat from * around, join with sl st to first sc. (36 sc)

Round 6: Ch 1, BPsc around each sc st in round, join with sl st to first BPsc. (36 BPsc)

Don't worry if the work seems to cup a little at this point. It will improve.

Round 7: Sk join st, *sk next st, 5 dc in next st, sk st, sl st in next st; repeat from * around, final sl st counts as join. (9 5-dc shells)

Turn piece over so back side is facing.

Round 8: *ch 5, sl st around BPsc between petals (This is the closest BPsc to where you placed your sl st. Working into actual sl sts will start in a few rounds); repeat from * around, final sl st counts as join. (9 ch-5 sp, 9 sl st)

Turn the piece back over so the right side is facing.

Round 9: *sl st into ch-5 sp, (hdc, 2 dc, 3 tr, 2 dc, hdc, sl st) in ch-5 sp; repeat from * around. Final sl st counts as join. (9 petals)

Round 10: Ch 1, *BPdc around next 3 sts, BPhdc around next 3 tr, BPdc around next 3 sts, sk 2 sl sts; repeat from * along each petal. Join with sl st to first BPdc. (54 Bpdc, 27 BPhdc)

Round 11: Ch 1, FPtr in sl st between first petals of round 7, *sk st, BPhdc around next 7 sts, sk st, (FPtr, ch 1, FPtr) in round 7 sl st between next 2 petals; repeat from * around omitting final FPtr. Join with sl st to first FPtr. (9 x 7-st petals, 18 FPtr, 9 ch-1 sps)

- From this point the piece should start laying flat.

Round 12: Ch 1, FPdc around FPtr, *ch 1, sk 2 sts, [3dc cluster in next st, ch 1] 3 times, sk 2 sts, FPdc around FPtr, ch 1, puff st in ch-1 sp, ch 1, FPdc around next FPtr; repeat from * around omitting final FPdc. Join with sl st to first FPdc. (18 FPdc, 9 puff sts, 27 3-dc clusters)

Round 13: Ch 1, *FPdc around FPdc, [sc in ch-1 sp, picot sc in top of 3 dc cluster] 3 times, sc in ch-1 sp, FPdc around FPdc, sk st (puff st, ch 1, puff st) in top of puff st from previous round, sk st; repeat from * around, join with sl st to first FPdc. (18 FPdc, 36 sc, 27 picot sc, 18 puff sts)

Round 14: ch 1, *FPsc around FPdc, [picot sc in next st, sc in next st] 3 times, picot sc in next st, FPsc around FPdc, sk to ch-1 sp between puff sts from previous round, 7 hdc in ch-1 sp; repeat from * around, join with sl st to first FPsc. (18 FPsc, 36 picot sc, 27 sc, 9 hdc petals)

Don't worry if the project puckers a bit after this round.

Round 15: Ch 1, *FPhdc around FPsc, [sc in next st, picot sc in next st] 3 times, sc in next st, FPhdc around FPsc, BPdc around next 7 hdc sts; repeat from * around, join with sl st to first FPhdc. (18 FPhdc, 9 BPdc petals, 36 sc, 27 picot sc)

Round 16: Ch 1, *FPhdc around FPhdc, sk 3 sts, 7 dc in next st, sk 3 sts, FPhdc around FPhdc, BPsc around next 7 sts; repeat from * around, join with sl st to first FPhdc. (144)

Round 17: Ch 1, *hdc in FPhdc, BPhdc around next 7 sts, hdc in FPhdc, hdc in next 7 sts; repeat from * around, join with sl st to first hdc. (144 hdc)

Round 18: Ch 1, BPsc in each st around, join with sl st to first BPsc. (144)

Round 19: Ch 1, [sc in next st, picot sc in next st] 6 times, sc in next st, hdc in next st, (3dc cluster, ch 1), in next st, *sk st, (3dc cluster, ch 1) in next st, sk st, (tr, ch 1, tr, ch 1) in next, sk st, (3dc cluster, ch 1) in next st, sk st, 3dc cluster in next st, hdc in next st, [sc in next st, picot sc in next st] 12 times, sc in next st, hdc in next st, (3dc cluster, ch 1) in next st; repeat from * around, ending final side with (tr, ch 1, tr, ch 1,) in next, sk st, (3dc cluster, ch 1) in next st, sk st, 3dc cluster in next st, hdc in next st, [sc in next st, picot sc in next st] 6 times, join with sl st to first sc. (Each side: 4 3dc clusters, 2 hdc, 2 tr, 13 sc, 12 picot sc)

The work should start flattening out at this point.

Round 20: Ch 1, sc in next 12 sts, *sk st, 5 dc in hdc, sc in ch-1 sp between 3dc clusters from previous round, skip next ch-1 sp, work (2tr cluster, ch 2, 2tr cluster, ch 2, 2tr cluster, ch 2, 2tr cluster) in next ch-1 sp, sc in ch-1 sp between 3dc clusters, 5 dc between hdc and sc sts from previous round, sk 2 sts, sc in next 22 sts; repeat from * around, omitting 12 sts at the end of final repeat, join with sl st to first sc. (Each side: 4 tr2tog, 2 5dc shells, 24 sc)

About the corners: The first tr2tog stitches worked in the corners of round 21 are worked around tr stitches and in the corner ch-1 space from round 19, 2 rounds below. This is the same ch-1 space where your 2tr clusters were worked in round 20. Although it's a lot of stitches to fit in a ch-1 space, it produces a neater corner. The two 'pillars' of the tr2tog are made over and around the 2tr clusters that were made in round 20. This should push the 2tr clusters from round 20 to the back. The tr2tog stitches in round 21 should both cover and flank the 2tr clusters from round 20 to give the petal its shape and create some dimension.

Round 21: Ch 1, BPsc around next 10 sts, *BPhdc around next 7 sts, BPdc around next sc, work tr2tog around first tr2tog made in previous round by working on the first tr from round 19 (2 rows below) and in ch-1 sp from round 19, 3 sc in first ch-2 sp between 2tr clusters in previous round, work tr2tog into the ch-1 sp from round 19 and around second 2tr cluster made in previous round, (2 hdc, ch 2, 2 hdc) in second ch-2 sp from previous round, tr2tog into ch-1 sp from round 19 and around third 2tr cluster made in previous round, 3 sc in third ch-2 sp, tr2tog around last 2tr cluster made in previous round by working first leg in ch-1 sp from round 19 and second leg around tr from round 19, BPdc around sc, BPhdc around next 7 sts, BPsc around next 18 sc; repeat from * omitting 10 BPsc on final repeat, join with sl st to first BPsc. (Each side: 18 BPsc, 14 BPhdc, 2 BPdc, 4 tr2tog, 6 sc, 4 hdc)

Round 22: Ch 1, sc in next 17 sts, *hdc in next 3 sts, sc in next 5 sts, (2 sc, ch 1, 2 sc) in ch-2 sp in corner, sc in next 5 sts (Note: The first 5 stitches you are working into will look like a chain, don't miss them), hdc in next

3 sts, sc in next 32 sts; repeat from * around, omitting 17 sts in final repeat, join with sl st to first sc. (Each side: 46 sc, 6 hdc)

Fasten off and weave in all ends.

Block to finish, if needed.

2. A Snowflake Story

A lacy snowflake is a quick item to make as a breather between more difficult ones. It comes together in only three rounds (Johanson, 2020).

Supplies needed:

- Some fingering weight yarn, depending on how many snowflakes you plan to make.
- Crochet hook, E-4 (3.5 mm)
- A blocking mat or a towel and pins
- A stiffening solution (optional)

Abbreviations:

- ch = chain

- ch # = ch # stitches, where # is the specified number of stitches
- dc = double crochet
- puff st = (yarn over hook, insert in st or sp, pull up a loop) three times, yarn over hook and pull through all 7 loops
- rep = repeat
- sc = single crochet
- sl st = slip stitch
- sp = space
- st(s) = stitch(es)
- tc = treble, or triple, crochet
- ( ) = repeat instructions within parentheses as directed
- [ ] = repeat instructions within brackets as directed

Gauge: It is not important for this project.

Specifics:

Diameter: 4 inches from tip to tip at the widest point.

If you use different yarn and a different size crochet hook, the size of the finished snowflake will change. That is an easy way to create a variety of sizes.

Several stitch patterns and shapes that require you to work into the same stitch several times are used. Read all the instructions carefully, noting where parentheses and brackets indicate groupings of stitches.

Puff stitches can be of different sizes depending on how many times you yarn over the hook and pull up a loop. In this pattern, the puff stitches are made with 7 loops on the hook.

Puff st = (yarn over hook, insert in st or sp, pull up a loop) three times, yarn over hook and pull through all 7 loops, ch 1 to finish the puff st.

Pattern:

Start: Make a slip knot and ch 6. Join with a sl st to form a ring.

Round 1: Ch 2 (counts as first sc plus ch-1 sp), [sc into the ring, ch 1] five times, sl st to first ch to join—12 sts. Crochet Round 1 with sc.

Round 2: Ch 4 (counts as first dc and ch-1 sp), [puff st in ch-1 sp, ch 1, dc in next st, ch 1] 5 times, puff st in ch-1 sp, ch 1, join to 3rd ch of first st with a sl st—6 puff sts, 6 dc sts. Crochet Round 2 with puff stitch and dc.

Making the snowflake points and branches

Note: The slip stitch at the start of the round moves the beginning of the round closer to the first puff stitch and that is where the snowflake points begin. When making the triangular points, work into the ch st sitting right on top of the puff.

Round 3: Sl st in ch-1 space, *[(dc, ch 1, tc); ch 3, sl st in 3rd ch from hook; (tc, ch 1, dc)] in ch 1 st that closes puff st, sk 1 st, [sl st, (ch 7, sl st in fifth, then sixth, then seventh ch from hook), sl st] in next dc, sk 2 sts; repeat from * 4 more times; [(dc, ch 1, tc); ch 3, sl st in 3rd ch from hook; (tc, ch 1, dc)] in ch 1 st that closes puff st, sk 1 st, [sl st, (ch 7, sl st in fifth, then sixth, then seventh ch from hook), sl st] in top of slip st at end of previous round—6 points, 6 branches.

Join with sl st into sl st of ch-1 space at beginning of round. Crochet Round 3 with sl st, dc, and tc.

Blocking

To show off the design of these snowflakes, block them as you would for any lace. You can even add some stiffening solution to help them keep their shape.

Soak the snowflakes in water or stiffening solution. Squeeze out as much of the water or solution as possible and pin them on a fluffy towel. Pull out and pin the triangular points first, then the rectangular branches, including the small loops at the ends of the branches.

Leave the snowflakes to dry completely.

Finishing: Add a thread hanger to one of the loops and hang them as Christmas decorations or give them away as gifts. They can also be used as appliques to stitch on a knit or crochet hat or scarf. If you add a felt backing and a pin at the back, you can turn them into brooches.

3. Diamonds Are Forever

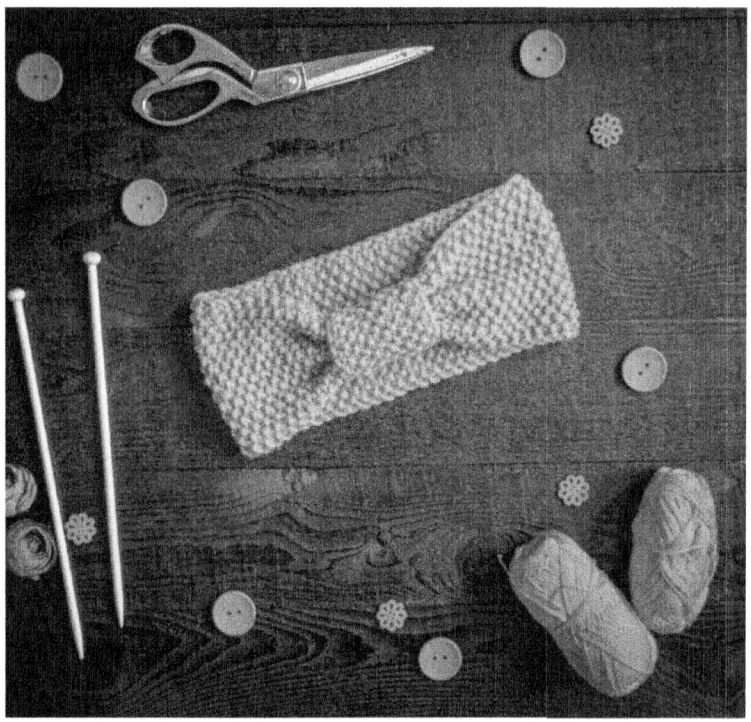

Beat the chilly winter breeze with a headband made with the lovely and versatile diamond stitch (Kent, 2016).

Supplies needed:

- 150 yards (2 skeins) of worsted yarn
- Crochet hook, 7 (4.5 mm)
- A tapestry needle
- Scissors

Abbreviations:

- st/s - stitch/es
- ch - chain stitch
- sl st - slip stitch
- sc - single crochet
- dc – double crochet
- fptr2tog – front post triple (treble) crochet 2 together

Gauge: 4 rows x 4 stitches in sc = 1 inch

Specifics:

The circumference is 20 inches and the width is 4 inches.

Front post triple/treble crochet 2 together (fptr2tog):

- Insert the hook into the next stitch. Yarn over, and pull back through that stitch (2 loops on hook).
- Insert the hook into the next stitch. Yarn over, and pull back through that stitch (3 loops on hook).
- Yarn over, and pull through all the loops on the hook.

Pattern:

Start: Ch 68. (Add or take away sets of 4 foundation chains if you'd like to create a smaller or larger headband). Join with sl st in first ch.

Round 1: Ch1, 1 sc in the same st. 1 sc in next 67 sts. Join with sl st in first st.

Round 2: Ch2, 1 dc in the same st. 1 dc in next 67 sts. Join with sl st in first st.

Round 3: Ch1, 1 sc in same st. 1 sc in next 2 sts. Fptr2tog around the 2nd sc from round 1 until 2 loops left on hook, skip 3 sc from round 1 and complete fptr2tog around next st from round 1. *1 sc in next 3 sts. Fptr2tog, working first part of fptr2tog around base of last fptr2tog, skip 3 sts (from round 1) and complete fptr2tog around next st from round 1. Repeat from * all around. When you reach last st, Fptr2tog, working first part of fptr2tog around base of last fptr2tog, skip 3 sts (from round 1), and complete fptr2tog around next st from round 1 (which is also the 2nd st of round 1). Join with sl st in first st of round 3.

Round 4: Ch2, 1 dc in the same st. 1 dc in the next 67 sts. Join with sl st in first st.

Round 5: Ch1, 1 sc in same st. Fptr2tog around top of last fptr2tog from round 3 (last st of that round) and first fptr2tog from round 3. *1 sc in next 3 sts of round 5. Fptr2tog, working first part of fptr2tog around tops of last fptr2tog you worked into from round 3, and then around next fptr2tog from round 3. Repeat from * all around. 1 sc in last 2 sts. Join with sl st in first st of round 5.

Round 6: Ch2, 1 dc in the same st. 1 dc in the next 67 sts. Join with sl st in first st.

Round 7: Ch1, 1 sc in same st. 1 sc in next 2 sts. Fptr2tog around top of first fptr2tog from round 5 (2nd st of "Rnd 5") and next fptr2tog from round 5. *1 sc in next 3 sts of round 7. Fptr2tog, working first part of fptr2tog around tops of last fptr2tog you worked into from round 5, and then around next fptr2tog from round 5. Repeat from * all around. When you reach last st, fptr2tog, working first part of fptr2tog around last fptr2tog you worked into from round 5, and complete fptr2tog around next fptr2tog from round 5 (which is also the 2nd st of round 5). Join with sl st in first st of round 7.

Round 8: Repeat round 4.

Round 9: Repeat round 5.

Round 10: Repeat round 6.

Round 11: Repeat round 7.

Round 12: Repeat round 4.

Round 13: Repeat round 5. (Add or take away sets of round 4 to round 7 if you'd like to create a thinner or wider headband).

Fasten off and weave in loose ends.

Border

Top: Attach the yarn to round 13 from the headband pattern. Ch1, sc all along the edge of the headband. Join with sl st in first st. (68 sts)

Fasten off and weave in loose ends.

Bottom

Attach the yarn to round 1 from the headband pattern. Ch1, sc all along the edge of the headband. Join with sl st in first st. (68 sts)

Fasten off and weave in loose ends.

4. A Tunisian Cowl

Tunisian crochet creates beautiful articles and this cowl in smock stitch is no exception to the rule (Halsey, 2020).

Supplies needed:

- 1 ball of bulky yarn (7 ounces)
- Tunisian crochet hook with cord, K-10.5 (6.5 mm)
- A yarn sewing needle
- Scissors
- Measuring tape

Abbreviations:

- ch - chain

- tks - Tunisian knit stitch
- tps - Tunisian purl stitch
- yu - yarn under
- yo - yarn over
- st/s - stitch/es
- tss2tog - Tunisian simple stitch decrease (see video tutorial here)
- tss - Tunisian simple stitch

Gauge: 11 stitches and 8 rows =4 inches

Specifics:

The finished size is 12.5 inches tall and 23 inches in circumference.

If you want to make the cowl taller, add more rows before adding the border. To make it wider, add as many chains (in multiples of 2) as needed to reach the desired length.

This pattern is worked flat with the right side of the work facing. It is seamed up the back when completed.

At the beginning of each row, the first stitch is on the hook and counts as a Tunisian knit stitch.

Do not turn the work at the beginning of each row. Each row is worked from right to left (forward pass) and then from left to right (return pass).

Pattern:

Row 1: Forward Pass: Ch 62, working into the back humps of each ch, pick up a loop in each ch across. (62)

Return Pass: Yo and pull through 1 loop on the hook, *yo and pull through 2 loops on the hook. Repeat from the * across until 1 loop remains on the hook. The length should measure approximately 23 inches.

Row 2: Forward Pass: Tks (on the hook), tps in each st across until 1 st remains, tks into the last st. (62)

Return Pass: Yo and pull through 1 loop on the hook, *yo and pull through 2 loops on the hook. Repeat from the * across until 1 loop remains on the hook.

Row 3: Repeat row 2. The fabric should measure approximately 1.75 inches tall.

Row 4: Forward Pass: Tks, *tss2tog, yu and hold the loop made to the side. Repeat from the * across until 1 st remains. tks into the last st. (62)

Return Pass: Yo and pull through 1 loop on the hook, *yo and pull through 2 loops on the hook. Repeat from the * across until 1 loop remains on the hook.

Row 5: Forward Pass: Tks, tss into the next st, *tss2tog, yu and hold the loop made to the side. Repeat from the * across until 2 sts remain. tss into the next st, tks into the last st. (62)

Return Pass: Yo and pull through 1 loop on the hook, *yo and pull through 2 loops on the hook. Repeat from the * across until 1 loop remains on the hook.

Row 6 to row 25: Repeat row 4 and row 5 or until 12 inches tall or until the desired length. The work should measure about 12 inches tall.

Row 26: Forward Pass: Tks (on the hook), tps in each st across until 1 st remains, tks into the last st. (62)

Return Pass: Yo and pull through 1 loop on the hook, *yo and pull through 2 loops on the hook. Repeat from the * across until 1 loop remains on the hook.

Row 27: Repeat row 26.

Finishing

*Insert the hook into the next st (just like for a tks), yo, and pull through all the loops on the hook to create a slip stitch. Repeat from the * across.

Seaming

Seam up the back of the cowl with any stitch you would like.

5. Celtic Stitch Blanket

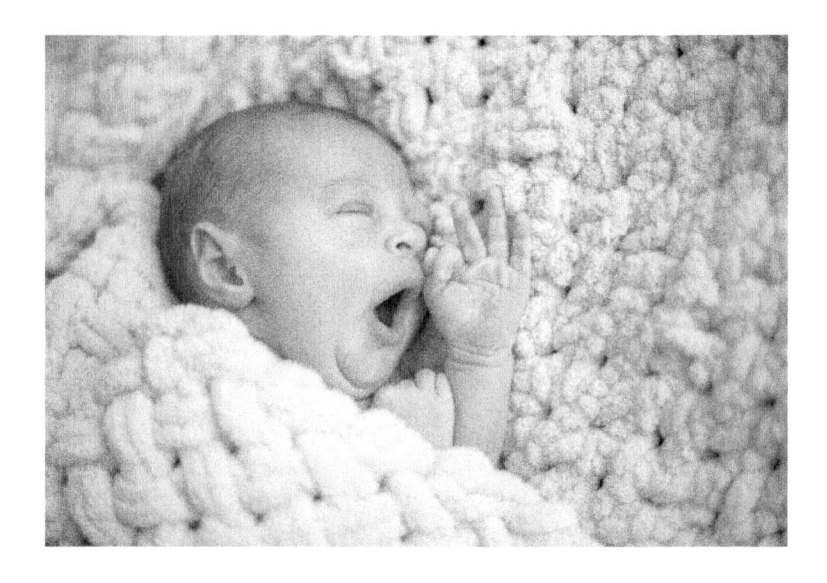

Celtic stitch with its weaved look is one of the most beautiful crochet stitches to use when making something that has to be warm, such as a blanket (Bittner, 2014).

Supplies needed:

- Any medium-weight/Aran yarn
- Crochet hook, H-8 (5 mm)

Abbreviations:

- ch = chain
- st/s =stitch/es
- sc = single crochet

- dc = double crochet
- bdc = beginning double crochet
- BPtc = back post treble crochet (yarn over 2 times, insert hook from back to front to back around the post of the stitch in previous row, yarn over and pull up loop (4 loops on hook), [yarn over, pull through two loops] 3 times).
- FPtc = front post treble crochet (yarn over 2 times, insert hook from front to back to front around the post of the stitch in previous row, yarn over and pull up loop (4 loops on hook), [yarn over, pull through two loops] 3 times).

Gauge: Not specified.

Specifics:

To change the size of the blanket, increase with a multiple of 4 chains (+ 3 chains) to turn, and that the beginning chain is the width the finished blanket should be, less 2 inches, to allow for a border if you will be adding one.

Every row is started with a dc instead of ch 3, to produce a sturdier beginning that will leave no gap.

Step 1: Draw the loop on the hook up somewhat, to about double its height.

Step 2: Hold that stitch tight at the bottom and on the top of the hook, and twist the hook down towards you, and then around to the back.

Step 3: Yo and bring the yarn through to the other side.

Step 4: Yo and draw the hook through both the loops on the hook.

Pattern:

Row 1: Start with a ch in a multiple of 4 and then add 3 ch, sc in 2nd ch from hook and each remaining ch (you should have an even number of sts), turn.

Row 2: Beginning dc, *skip 2, FPtc in next 2 sts, crossing in front of two FPtc just made, work FPtc in two skipped sts*. Repeat between * to end, dc in last st, turn.

Row 3: Working from back, bdc, BPtc first 2 sts, *skip 2, BPtc next 2 sts, crossing behind last two BPtc made, BPtc in two skipped sts*. Repeat between * to last 3 sts. Work BPtc in next two sts, dc in last st, turn.

Row 4: Bdc, *skip 2, FPtc in next 2, crossing in front of two FPtc just made, work FPtc in two skipped sts*. Repeat between * to end, dc in last st, turn.

Repeat rows 3 and 4 until blanket measures desired length, ending with row 4.

Border

Round 1: *Ch 1, work 3 sc in corner, work sc evenly across side to next corner*; repeat between * to end, join with sl st to bsc. (Note: St count between center corner sts must be divisible by 6, + 1 extra st) (Example: 19, 31, 37, 43, etc).

Round 2: Ch 1, sc in same st, [*7dc in next st (this should be the center st of the corner), *sc in next st, skip 2, 5dc in next st, skip 2*; repeat between * to st before the corner, sc in st before the corner]; repeat between [and] to end, join with sl st to bsc.

Fasten off and weave in all ends.

6. Cables to Keep You Warm

Beat the cold with a cozy wrap made in a cabled pattern (Wilson, 2010).

Supplies needed:

- 7 skeins of medium-weight/Aran yarn
- Crochet hook, I-9 (5.5 mm)
- Crochet hook, J-10 (6 mm)
- A yarn sewing needle
- Row counter (optional)

Abbreviations:

- ch = chain
- dc = double crochet

- sc = single crochet
- tr = treble crochet
- st/s = stitch/es
- FPdc = Front Post double crochet (Yarn over, insert hook from front to back to front around st indicated, yarn over and pull up loop, [yarn over and draw through 2 loops] twice).
- FPtr = Front Post treble crochet (Yarn over, insert hook from front to back to front around st indicated, yarn over and pull up loop, [yarn over and draw through 2 loops] 3 times).
- RT = Right Twist (Skip next sc, FPdc around next 3 dc, sc in sc behind previous FPdc).
- LT = Left Twist (Sc in next sc, FPdc around next 3 dc).
- RS = right side
- WS = wrong side

Gauge: 14 sts and 17 rows = 4 inches with larger hook but gauge is not critical for this project.

Specifics:

Unless instructed otherwise, skip sc behind FPdc.

Cable: Skip 2 FPdc, FPtr around each of next 2 FPdc, FPtr around each of 2 skipped FPdc.

Pattern:

Start: Ch 84 using smaller hook.

Row 1 (RS): Dc in 4th ch from hook and in each ch across, turn, change to larger hook. (82 dc)

Row 2 and every WS row: Ch 1, sc in each st across, turn.

Row 3: Ch 1, sc, 4 FPdc, sc, (3 FPdc, 8 sc, 3 FPdc) 5 times, sc, 4 FPdc, sc, turn.

Row 5: Ch 1, sc, cable, sc, (LT, 6 sc, RT) 5 times, sc, cable, sc, turn.

Row 7: Ch 1, sc, 4 FPdc, sc, (sc, LT, 4 sc, RT, sc) 5 times, sc, 4 FPdc, sc, turn.

Row 9: Ch 1, sc, cable, sc, (2 sc, LT, 2 sc, RT, 2 sc) 5 times, sc, cable, sc, turn.

Row 11: Ch 1, sc, 4 FPdc, sc, (3 sc, LT, RT, 3 sc) 5 times, sc, 4 FPdc, sc, turn.

Row 13: Ch 1, sc, cable, sc, (4 sc, 6 FPdc, 4 sc,) 5 times, sc, cable, sc, turn.

Row 15: Ch 1, sc, 4 FPdc, sc, (3 sc, RT, LT, 3 sc) 5 times, sc, 4 FPdc, sc, turn.

Row 17: Ch 1, sc, cable, sc, (2 sc, RT, 2 sc, LT, 2 sc) 5 times, sc, cable, sc, turn.

Row 19: Ch 1, sc, 4 FPdc, sc, (sc, RT, 4 sc, LT, sc) 5 times, sc, 4 FPdc, sc, turn.

Row 21: Ch 1, sc, cable, sc, (RT, 6 sc, LT) 5 times, sc, cable, sc, turn.

Row 22: Ch 1, sc in each st across, turn.

Rows 23 to 282: Repeat Rows 3 to 22.

Row 283: Repeat row 3.

Fasten off.

Finishing

Start at corner st and work 3 sc in same st with larger hook, * working across long edge of piece, sc in every other row to corner, work 3 sc in corner, sc in each st across short edge), work 3 sc in corner; repeat from * once on remaining 2 sides; join with slip st to first st.

Fasten off and weave in all ends.

7. An Elegant Poncho With Heart Detail

The enjoyable challenge in this poncho does not lie in the pattern as such but rather in the folded-down collar and folded-up hem with heart detail that give the garment a very elegant finish (Thadani, 2015).

Supplies needed:

- 6 skeins of medium-weight/Aran yarn in the main color
- 1 skein of medium-weight/Aran yarn in another color
- Crochet hook, J-10 (6 mm)
- A yarn sewing needle
- Stitch marker/safety pins

Abbreviations:

- RS = right side
- ch = chain
- sc = single crochet
- dc = double crochet
- sl st = slip stitch
- st/s = stitch/es
- sp/s = space/s
- sk = skip
- sc2tog = single crochet 2 stitches together
- dc2tog = double crochet 2 stitches together
- dc3tog = double crochet 3 stitches together
- long dc = long double crochet
- heart = heart stitch

Gauge: 12 dc x 7 rows = approximately 4 inches square. The narrowest point at row 6 should be about 22 inches long.

Specifics:

One size fits most people.

Heart stitch:

Work (2dc, ch1, 2dc) all in the same st.

Long double crochet:

Work the same as a normal dc, except when drawing up a loop, pull it up a bit higher than normal so that the stitches come out to the height of the current row.

Notes:

The right and wrong sides will change because the collar and hem are flipped over. On these two parts, the odd-numbered rows are RS rows. On the main part of the poncho, the even-numbered rows are the RS rows.

Stitch counts shown do not include the corner chain 2 spaces.

Starting ch 3 counts as the first dc. Starting ch 1 or ch 2 does NOT count as a stitch.

In row 3b of the collar and round 53b of the hem, the long dc stitches are worked over the chains in the secondary color, so they are hidden within the dc stitches.

Add rounds between rounds 43 and 44 to make the poncho longer. Any addition has to be in sets of 4 (repeats of rounds 10 to 13).

The multiples to keep in mind (not counting the corner chain spaces) are:

Row 1 has a multiple of 12 + 10 stitches, so the starting chain is a multiple of 12 + 3.

Row 2 (to set up for the heart stitch row) should be a multiple of 12 + 5.

Round 43 (to set up for the heart stitch round) should be a multiple of 12 + 4.

Round 57 should have the same number of stitches as round 43.

Pattern:

Collar

Start: Ch 87.

Row 1 (RS): Sc2tog in 2nd and 3rd ch from hook, sc in next 40 chs, sk next 2 chs, sc in next 40 chs, sc2tog in last 2 ch, turn. (82 sts)

Row 2: Ch 2, sk first st, dc in next 38 sts, dc2tog, ch 2 (corner), dc3tog, dc in next 36 sts, dc2tog, turn. Secure working loop with stitch marker to stop it from pulling out and removing hook. (77 sts)

Row 3a: Skip first 4 sts, join 2nd color with sl st in 5th st. [Ch 3 (counts as dc, now and throughout), (dc, ch1, 2dc) in same sp, (ch 4, sk next 5 sts, heart in next st) 5 times], fasten off 2nd color – there should be 3 unworked sts left before corner. Join 2nd color with sl st in 5th st after ch sp, repeat between [ ], fasten off 2nd color, leaving last 4 sts unworked. Do not turn. (12 hearts)

Row 3b: Pick up the main color loop that was set aside at the end of row 2. Ch 2, sk first st, long dc in next 2 sts, [ch 1, sc in ch sp at top of heart, (ch 1, sk the dc just after heart, working over the 2nd color chain, long dc in next 3 dc, ch 1, sc in ch sp at top of heart) 5 times, ch 1, sk the dc just after the heart], dc2tog being sure to draw loops up to row height just like for the long dc, ch 2, sk ch sp, dc3tog being sure to draw loops up to row height, repeat between [ ],dc in next st, dc2tog being sure to draw loops up to row height, turn.

Row 4: Ch 2, sk first st, dc in next dc, dc in next ch sp, (dc in next sc, dc in next ch sp, dc in next 3dc, dc in next ch sp) 5 times, dc in next sc, dc2tog using the next ch sp and the following st, ch2, sk ch sp, (dc3tog using the next st, ch sp, and following st), (dc in next ch sp, dc in next 3 dc, dc in next ch sp, dc in next sc) 5 times, dc in last ch sp, dc2tog, turn. (67 sts)

Row 5: Ch 1, sc2tog, sc in next 31 sts, ch 2, sk ch sp, sc2tog, sc in next 30 sts, sc2tog changing to 2nd color, turn, fasten off main color. (64 sts)

Row 6: With 2nd color, ch 1, sc in next 32 sts, ch 2, sk ch sp, sc in next 32 sts changing to main color with last st, turn, fasten off 2nd color. Mark last st of this row for edging.

Poncho

Row 7: With main color, and working in BLO: Ch 3, 2dc in same st, dc in next 31 sts, (dc, ch 2, 2dc) in ch sp, dc in next 31 sts, 2dc in last st, turn (70 sts).

Round 8 (RS): Work in both loops as normal: Ch 3, 2dc in same st, dc in next 34 sts, (dc, ch 2, 2dc) in ch sp, dc in next 34 sts, 2dc in last st, ch 2, join with sl st in top of starting ch 3 to begin working in rounds, turn. (76 sts)

Round 9: Sl st in ch sp, ch 3, dc in same sp, dc in each st across to next ch sp, (dc, ch 2, 2dc) in ch sp, dc in each st across, dc in same ch sp as start of round, ch 2, join, turn. (82 sts)

Round 10: Sl st in ch sp, ch 3, dc in same sp, [(ch 1, sk next st, dc in next 2 sts) across to last 2 sts before ch sp, ch 1, sk next st, dc in next st], (dc, ch 2, 2dc) in ch sp, repeat between [ ], dc in same ch sp as start of round, ch 2, join, turn. (60 sts)

Round 11: Sl st in corner ch sp, ch 3, dc in same sp, dc in each ch 1 sp and in each dc across to next corner, (dc, ch 2, 2dc) in corner ch sp, dc in each ch 1 sp and in each dc across, dc in same corner ch sp as start of round, ch 2, join, turn. (94 sts)

Round 12 to 13: Sl st in ch sp, ch 3, dc in same sp, dc in each st across to next ch sp, (dc, ch 2, 2dc) in ch sp, dc in each st across, dc in same ch sp as start of round, ch 2, join, turn. (106 sts)

Rounds 14 to 43: Repeat rounds 10-13 seven more times, then repeat rounds 10 and 11 once more. (286 sts)

Round 44: Working in BLO: Sl st in corner ch sp, dc in 2nd ch of same ch sp, dc in each dc across to next corner, dc in next ch, ch 2, 2dc in next ch, dc in each st across, dc in first ch of same ch sp as start of round, ch 2, join, turn. (292 sts)

Round 45: Work in both loops as normal: Repeat round 13. (298 sts)

Rounds 46 to 48: Repeat rounds 10 to 12 of poncho. (316 sts)

Hem

Round 49 (RS): Working in BLO: Sl st in corner ch sp, sl st in first st, changing to 2nd color. Fasten off main color. With 2nd color, ch 1, sc2tog in same st and next st, [sc in each st across to corner, ch 2, sk ch sp], sc2tog, repeat between [ ], join, turn. (314 sts)

Round 50: Working in both loops as normal: Sl st in corner ch sp, sl st in first sc changing to main color. Fasten off 2nd color. With main color, ch 1, [sc2tog, sc in each st across to 2 sts before corner, sc2tog, ch 2], sk ch sp, repeat between [ ], join, turn. (310 sts)

Round 51: Sl st in corner ch sp, sl st in first st, ch 1, [sc in each st across to 2 sts before corner, sc2tog, ch 2], sk ch sp, repeat between [ ], join, turn. (308 sts)

Round 52: Sl st in corner ch sp, sl st in first st, ch 1, [sc2tog, sc in each st across to 2 sts before corner, sc2tog, ch 2], sk ch sp, repeat between [ ], join, turn. Secure working loop with stitch marker so it can't pull out, and remove hook. (304 sts)

Round 53a: Skip ch sp and first 3 sts, join 2nd color with sl st in 4th st. [Ch 3 (counts as dc, now and throughout), (dc, ch1, 2dc) in same sp, ch 4, sk next 5 sts, (heart in next st, ch 4, sk next 5 sts) 24 times], fasten off 2nd color—there should be 4 unworked sts left before corner. Join 2nd color with sl st in 4th st after ch sp, repeat between [ ], fasten off 2nd color, leaving last 4 sts unworked. Do not turn. (50 hearts)

Round 53b: Pick up main color loop that was set aside at end of round 4. Ch 2, sk first st, long dc in next st, [ch 1, (sc in ch sp at top of heart, ch 1, sk the sc just after the heart, working over 2nd color chain, long dc in next 3 sc, ch 1,) 24 times, sc in ch sp at top of heart, ch 1, sk the sc just after the heart, dc3tog being sure to draw loops up to row height just like for long dc, ch 2], sk ch sp, dc2tog being sure to draw loops up to row height, repeat [ ], join, turn.

Round 54: Sl st in corner ch sp, sl st in first st, ch 1, [sc2tog, sc in each st across to 2 sts before corner, sc2tog, ch 2], sk ch sp, repeat between [ ], join, turn. (296 sts)

Round 55: Sl st in corner ch sp, sl st in first st, ch 1, [sc in each st across to 2 sts before corner, sc2tog, ch 2], sk ch sp, repeat between [ ], join, turn. (292 sts)

Round 56: Repeat round 54. (290 sts)

Round 57: Sl st in corner ch sp, sl st in first sc, changing to 2nd color, fasten off main color. With 2nd color, ch 1, [sc2tog, sc in each st across to corner, ch 2] sk ch sp, repeat between [ ], join, turn. (286 sts)

Joining

Weave any loose ends in the hem area in before joining. Hem should fold up naturally, just ensure corner ch sps are lined up. Working through both loops of round 57 and unused loops from round 43, sl st in 2nd ch of ch sp, sl st in each st, and ch around.

Fasten off.

Edging

Bottom: With RS facing, join 2nd color with sl st in either corner chain space on the bottom edge of the poncho. Working in unused loops from row 48, (ch1, sl in next st) across to corner, (ch1, sl, ch1, sl) in corner, (Ch1, sl in next st) across to the corner you started in, (ch1, sl, ch1) in corner, sl to 1st st, fasten off.

Collar: With RS facing, join 2nd color in marked st (last st on row 6). Working in sides of rows, work 4 sc evenly spaced to the corner of the collar (row 1). Working in bottom of row 1, 3 sc in first st, sc in each st across to last st, 3sc in last st. Working in sides of rows, work 8 sc evenly spaced to the bottom of the neckline. Working in sides of rows, work 4 sc evenly spaced back to marked st, join with sl st to first st of edging, fasten off. Weave in all ends.

8. Bruges Lace Border

This beautiful type of lace that had its origins in Brugge, Belgium in the 16th century imitates the lace that is made on bobbins. It consists of several pieces that are joined to form one exquisitely filigreed fabric. This pattern has a wave strip, a straight strip, and a picot row (Rubarge, 2017).

Supplies needed:

- 1 ball of size 10 mercerized cotton thread, 700-46
- 1 ball of size 10 mercerized cotton thread, 700-31

- Steel crochet hook, size 8 (1.5 mm)
- A yarn sewing needle

Abbreviations:

- ch = chain
- st/s = stitch/es
- dc = double crochet
- dc-tr = double crochet-treble crochet
- tr-dc = treble crochet-double crochet
- sp/s = space/s
- lp = loop
- beg = beginning
- rem = remaining

Gauge: Although gauge is not critical, 9 rows on straight strip at widest part = 2 inches x 2 inches.

Specifics:

The finished size is 2 inches at the widest part and the length is adjustable.

The edging is made of three consecutive parts: A wave strip, a straight strip, and a picot row. Work the wave strip to the approximate required length. Do not fasten off. Secure the thread temporarily by placing a stitch marker in the last loop.

With a separate ball, work the straight strip from the beginning of the wave strip, attaching to the wave strip at the same time. Adjust the length of both the wave strip and straight strip as needed. Continue to work the picot lace row from the released wave strip thread.

If handling multiple strands is not convenient, make the strips somewhat longer than needed, fasten off, and adjust the length by ravelling at the end as necessary.

Suggested edging end allows for about 1-inch overlap/seam margin.

Sc in 3 ch-6 sps: Insert hook in each sp from front to back at same time, yo and draw yarn through all 3 sps, yo and draw through 2 rem lps.

Dc-tr cluster: Yo, insert hook in same ch-6 sp, yo and pull up lp, yo and draw through 2 lps (2 lps rem on hook), yo 2 times, insert hook in sc over center ch-6 sp, yo and pull up lp, [yo, draw through 2 lps] 2 times, yo and draw through 3 rem lps.

Tr-dc cluster: Yo 2 times, insert hook in same sc over center ch-6 sp, yo and pull up lp, [yo, draw through 2 lps] 2 times (2 lps rem on hook), yo, insert hook in next ch-6 sp, yo and pull up lp, yo and draw through 2 lps, yo and draw through 3 rem lps.

Picot: Ch 3, insert hook through front lp and left vertical bar of base st, yo and draw through all lps on hook.

Pattern:

Wave strip

Start: Ch 10.

Row 1: Dc in 7th ch from hook, dc in next 3 ch, turn—4 dc.

Row 2: Ch 6, dc in each dc, turn.

Rows 3 to 8: Rep row 2. Do not turn at end of row 8.

Row 9: Ch 3, sc in 3 ch-6 sps just made on side of rows, ch 3, turn, dc in each dc, turn.

Rep rows 3 to 9 for patt.

Finish

Rep row 2 three times (or as many as desired). Secure thread. Do not fasten off.

Straight strip (joining to wave strip at the same time)

Start: Ch 8.

Row 1: Dc in 5th ch from hook, dc in next 3 ch to 4 dc.

Row 2: Ch 3, sl st in first ch-6 sp on inner side of wave strip (beg of strip), ch 3, turn, dc in each dc, turn.

Rows 3, 5, 7, 9, 11: Ch 4, dc in each dc.

Row 4: Ch 3, dc-tr cluster, ch 3, turn, dc in each dc, turn.

Row 6: Ch 3, tr-dc cluster, ch 3, turn, dc in each dc, turn.

Row 8: Ch 3, sl st in same ch-6 sp, ch 3, turn, dc in each dc, turn.

Row 10: Ch 3, sl st in next ch-6 sp (top of wave), ch 3, turn, dc in each dc, turn.

Rep rows 2 to 11 for patt.

Finish

Rep rows 2 to 6 working in second to last ch-6 sp instead of sc on last rep.

Picot lace edge

Release secured thread at end of wave strip, ch 3, sc in first inner ch-6 sp on wave strip, picot, ch 6, *sc in sc over center ch-6 sp, picot, ch 6, (sc, picot, ch 6) in next 3 ch-6 sps; rep from * to last picot, ch 3, sl st in beg ch of wave strip.

Finishing

Weave in ends.

To block, iron on cotton setting through wet cheesecloth or soak, pin, and let dry.

9. A Classic Capelet in Broomstick Lace

Broomstick lace, which is also sometimes called jiffy lace, uses a crochet hook as well as a long, thin bar to hold the stitches that are picked up with the hook from the base row. In this pattern, a knitting needle does the job that was done by a broomstick in the 19th century, when the technique was developed (Pullen, 2007).

Supplies needed:

- 4 balls of lace-weight bouclé yarn
- Steel crochet hook, 4 (2 mm)
- Steel crochet hook, 9 (3.5 mm)
- Knitting needle, size 19 (15 mm)

- A tapestry needle
- Scissors

Abbreviations:

- ch = chain
- st/s = stitch/es
- lp/s = loop/s
- yo = yarn over
- rep = repeat
- RS = right side
- WS = wrong side

Gauge: 4½ eyes and 4½ rows = 4 inches.

Specifics:

The pattern is for sizes 32–34 (36–38, 40–42) inches around the neck edge.

Don't pull the yarn too tightly at the beginning of a row, to avoid distortion.

The "broomstick needle" should be held firmly. Put it under your arm or clamp it between your knees. Work the loops onto the needle with a smaller crochet hook that fits into the loops easily.

Thread thin ribbon through the stitches at the top to gather slightly, or stitch elastic to the back, to tighten the neckline for narrow shoulders.

Increase or decrease the length of the capelet by working more or fewer rows prior to shaping.

The garment is worked flat and then seamed.

How to do broomstick crochet:

Each row of this technique is worked in two steps without turning; the RS is always facing.

Start with a foundation equal to the number of sts required (in this example, we use a multiple of 5 sts). Do not turn work.

Row 1, first pass: Enlarge lp on hook and place on broomstick, *insert hook in next st or ch to the right if right-handed (in next st or ch to the left if left-handed), pull up a long lp, and place on broomstick; rep from * to the end of the row. There is one lp on broomstick for every st or ch. Do not turn work.

Row 1, second pass: Insert hook through 5 lps on broomstick, yo, draw through all 5 lps, ch 1, sl group off broomstick, work 5 sc in center of group, *insert hook through next 5 lps on broomstick, yo, draw through all 5 lps, yo, draw through both lps on hook (first sc made), work 4 sc in center of group; rep from * to end of row. Do not turn work.

Repeat steps 2 and 3 for broomstick lace pattern.

How to decrease broomstick crochet:

At beg of second pass, insert hook through 10 lps on broomstick, yo, draw through all 10 lps, ch 1, sl group off broomstick, work 5 sc in center of group (1 eye dec'd).

Pattern:

Start: With larger hook, ch 280 (300, 320).

Row 1, first pass: Enlarge lp on hook and place it on the broomstick, *insert hook in next st or ch to the right if right-handed (in next st or ch to the left if left-handed), pull up a long lp, and place on broomstick; rep from * to the end of the row. There is one lp on broomstick for every st or ch. Do not turn.

Row 1, second pass: Insert hook through 5 lps on broomstick, yo, draw through all 5 lps, ch 1, sl group off broomstick, work 5 sc in center of group, *insert hook through next 5 lps on broomstick, yo, draw through all 5 lps, yo, draw through both lps on hook (first sc made), work 4 sc in center of group; rep from * to the end of the row. Do not turn. (56 (60, 64) eyes)

Rep first and 2nd pass of row 1 a total of 16 times.

Dec row 1: Pick up lps in the normal manner, *work 10 (11, 12) eyes, [broomstick dec over next 10 lps] twice; rep from *.

Dec row 2: Pick up lps in the normal manner, *work 10 (11, 12) eyes, broomstick dec over next 10 lps; rep from * to end. Note: This dec works 2 eyes that were dec'd in previous row tog and forms a dart. (44 (48, 52) eyes)

Top band: With larger hook, work 5 rows of sc. Change to smaller hook, work 6 rows of sc. Change to larger hook, work (sc, ch 1, sc) in each st of previous row.

Fasten off.

Finishing

Invisible joining: With WS facing and darning needle, seam the work on the sc row of the broomstick crochet, then thread the yarn through the next eye to bring it to the next st. Weave in loose ends by threading through sts at the back of the garment.

Block gently.

10. Tapestry Crochet Afghan Square

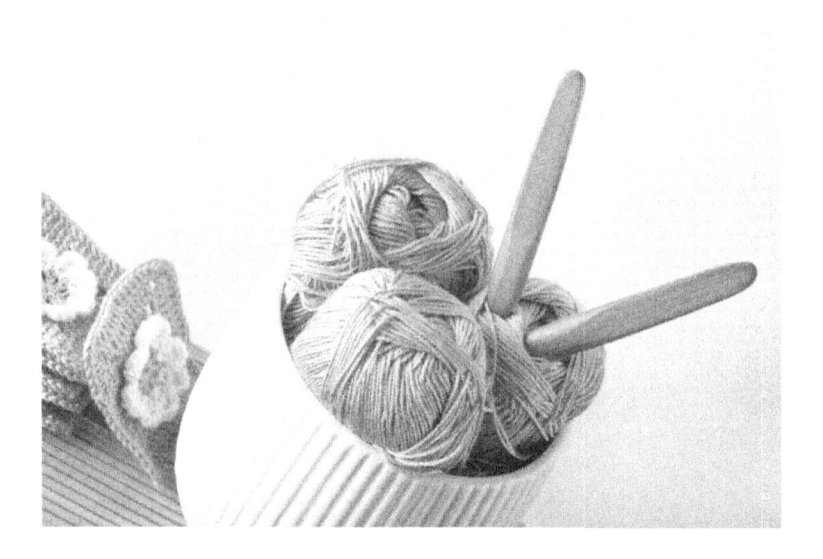

In tapestry crochet, two colors are used. The unused yarn is not cut but rather carried along behind the work and woven into the stitches, creating a tapestry-like effect. You can either make an afghan of similar squares or use a variety of patterns to make up the end result. This pattern was designed with red hearts on cream as the main color (Ventura, 1991).

Supplies needed:

- 140 yards of worsted-weight yarn in a cream color
- 140 yards of worsted-weight yarn in a red color

- Crochet hook, N-15 (10 mm) (adjust if necessary to obtain the right gauge)
- A stitch marker

Abbreviations:

- ch = chain
- st/s = stitch/es
- dc = double crochet
- sl st = slip stitch
- lp/s = loop/s
- pm = place marker
- B = cream color yarn
- F = red color yarn

Gauge: 12½ sts and 11 rows = 4 inches

Specifics:

The finished size is 12 inches by 12 inches.

The square is worked as a spiral, do not join at the end of a round.

To carry a color, lay it over top 2 lps of sts being worked in and work st as usual, placing the carried color inside st being worked.

With tapestry crochet, 1 color is worked in sc while another is carried. Colors are switched while 2 lps of st rem; yo with 2nd color and pull it through the 2 lps. Untwist the yarn at the end of each round.

Pattern:

Start: With B ch 4, sl st in first ch to form a ring.

Round 1: 7 sc in ring carrying tail, pull tail to tighten. (7 sc)

Round 2: Cont to carry tail and beg to carry F, with B sc in first sc, 2 sc in next 6 sc, pm in last sc to mark end of round. (13 sts)

Round 3: Cut tail, with B sc in next sc, [sc in next 2 sc, (sc, ch 2, sc) in next st] 4 times, pm in corner ch (move m up at end of each Round). (7 sc and 4 ch-2 sps)

Round 4: [With F sc in next sc, with B sc in next 3 sc, (sc, ch 2, sc) in corner ch-2 sp] 4 times. (4 sc and 4 ch-2 sps)

Round 5: [With B sc in next sc, with F sc in next 2 sc, with B sc in next 3 sc, (sc, ch 2, sc) in corner ch-2 sp] 4 times. (32 sc and 4 ch-2 sps)

Round 6: [With B sc in next 2 sc, with F sc in next 3 sc, with B sc in next 3 sc, (sc, ch 2, sc) in corner ch-2 sp] 4 times. (40 sc and 4 ch-2 sps)

Round 7: [With B sc in next 2 sc, with F sc in next 5 sc, with B sc in next 3 sc, (sc, ch 2, sc) in corner ch-2 sp] 4 times. (78 sc and 4 ch-2 sps)

Round 8: [With B sc in next 3 sc, with F sc in next 6 sc, with B sc in next 3 sc, (sc, ch 2, sc) in corner ch-2 sp] 4 times. (56 sc and 4 ch-2 sps)

Round 9: [With B sc in next 3 sc, with F sc in next 8 sc, with B sc in next 3 sc, (sc, ch 2, sc) in corner ch-2 sp] 4 times. (64 sc and 4 ch-2 sps)

Round 10: [With B sc in next 4 sc, with F sc in next 9 sc, with B sc in next 3 sc, (sc, ch 2, sc) in corner ch-2 sp] 4 times. (72 sc and 4 ch-2 sps)

Round 11: [With B sc in next 4 sc, with F sc in next 11 sc, with B sc in next 3 sc, (sc, ch 2, sc) in corner ch-2 sp] 4 times. (80 sc and 4 ch-2 sps)

Round 12: [With B sc in next 5 sc, with F sc in next 12 sc, with B sc in next 3 sc, (sc, ch 2, sc) in corner ch-2 sp] 4 times. (88 sc and 4 ch-2 sps)

Round 13: [With B sc in next 7 sc, with F sc in next 5 sc, with B sc in next sc, with F sc in next 5 sc, with B sc in next 4 sc, (sc, ch 2, sc) in corner ch-2 sp] 4 times. (96 sc and 4 ch-2 sps)

Round 14: [With B sc in next 9 sc, with F sc in next 4 sc, with B sc in next 2 sc, with F sc in next 4 sc, with B sc in next 5 sc, (sc, ch 2, sc) in corner ch-2 sp] 4 times. (104 sc and 4 ch-2 sps)

Round 15: [With B sc in next 11 sc, with F sc in next 3 sc, with B sc in next 3 sc, with F sc in next 3 sc, with B sc in next 6 sc, (sc, ch 2, sc) in corner ch-2 sp] 4 times. (112 sc and 4 ch-2 sps)

Round 16: [With B sc in next 28 sc, (sc, ch 2, sc) in corner ch-2 sp] 4 times. (120 sc and 4 ch-2 sps.

Round 17: [With B sc in next 30 sc, (sc, ch 2, sc) in corner] 4 times, fasten off F, with B sl st in next st. (128 sc and 4 ch-2 sps)

Fasten off B.

Steam to block.

11. A Flowing Butterfly Cardigan

This lacy shell stitch pattern makes a soft, loose cardigan that ties together at the bottom. It is made in three pieces from the bottom up and the sleeves are shaped to carry the flowing, loose feeling. The whole garment is crocheted with two threads together (Redheart, 2021).

Supplies needed:

- 6 (6, 7, 8, 9, 11, 12) balls of crochet thread
- Crochet hook, F-5 (3.75 mm)
- A yarn needle
- Stitch markers

Abbreviations:

- ch = chain
- st/s = stitch/es
- dc = double crochet
- tr = treble crochet
- yo = yarn over
- Y-st = Y stitch
- tr-dc-tog = treble-double crochet 2 stitches together

Gauge: 17 sts = 4 inches; 9 rows = 4 inches while the piece is crocheted. Each sc, dc, tr, and ch-1 space count as one st.

The piece will stretch as it progresses and the final, blocked gauge will be closer to 3 stitch pattern repeats = 4 inches; 8 rows = 5 inches, where one stitch pattern repeat consists of one shell and the following sc and ch-1 spaces.

Specifics:

The directions are for size Extra Small. To change to sizes Small, Medium, Large, 1X, 2X, and 3X, read the numbers in parentheses.

Hip measurement: 34 (36, 42, 44, 47, 52, 55) inches.

Finished hip measurement: 35 (37, 43, 45, 48, 53, 56) inches.

Shell: (Dc, ch 1, tr, ch 1, dc) in indicated stitch or space.

Y stitch: Tr in indicated stitch, ch 1, dc in base of tr just made. Note: To insert hook in base of tr, insert the hook into the tr between the stitch the tr was worked into and the first horizontal bar of the tr.

Treble-double crochet 2 stitches together: [Yarn over] twice, insert hook in next stitch, yarn over and pull up a loop, [yarn over and draw through 2 loops on hook] twice (2 loops remain on hook), yarn over, insert hook in next stitch, yarn over and pull up a loop, yarn over and draw through 2 loops on hook, yarn over and draw through all 3 loops on hook.

Pattern:

Back

Start: With 2 strands of thread held together, ch 83 (89, 101, 107, 113, 125, 131).

Row 1 (right side): Dc in 5th ch from hook, ch 1, skip next 2 ch, sc in next ch, *ch 1, skip next 2 ch, shell in next ch, ch 1, skip next 2 ch, sc in next ch; repeat from

* to last 3 ch, ch 1, skip next 2 ch, (dc, ch 1, tr) in last ch, turn. (12 (13, 15, 16, 17, 19, 20) shells)

Row 2: Ch 1, sc in first tr, *ch 1, Y-st in next sc, ch 1, sc in next tr; repeat from * across working last sc in 4th ch of turning ch, turn.

Row 3: Ch 1, sc in first sc, *ch 1, skip next ch-1 space, shell in next ch-1 space (at center of Y-st), ch 1, sc in next sc; repeat from * across, turn. (13 (14, 16, 17, 18, 20, 21) shells)

Row 4: Ch 4 (counts as tr), dc in 4th ch from hook, ch 1, sc in next tr, *ch 1, Y-st in next sc, ch 1, sc in next tr; repeat from * to last sc, ch 1, tr in last sc, dc in base of tr just made, turn.

Row 5: Ch 5, dc in first dc, ch 1, sc in next sc, *ch 1, skip next ch-1 space, shell in next ch-1 space, ch 1, sc in next sc; repeat from * to the last ch-1 space, ch 1, skip last ch-1 space, (dc, ch 1, tr) on top of turning ch, turn. (12 (13, 15, 16, 17, 19, 20) shells)

Rows 6–9 (9, 9, 13, 13, 17, 17): Repeat last 4 rows 1 (1, 1, 2, 2, 3, 3) more times.

Shape sleeves

Row 1 (wrong side): Ch 7, sc in 2nd ch from hook and place marker in sc just made (for seaming), sc in next 5 ch, sc in next tr, *ch 1, Y-st in next sc, ch 1, sc in next tr; repeat from * across working last sc in 4th ch of turning ch, turn.

Row 2: Ch 7, sc in 2nd ch from hook and place marker in sc just made (for seaming), ch 1, skip next 2 ch, shell in next ch, ch 1, skip next 2 ch, sc in next sc, *ch 1, skip next ch-1 space, shell in next ch-1 space, ch 1, sc in next sc; repeat from * to last 6 sc, ch 1, skip next 2 sc, shell in next sc, ch 1, skip next 2 sc, sc in last sc, turn. (15 (16, 18, 19, 20, 22, 23) shells)

Row 3: Ch 8, sc in 2nd ch from hook and in next 3 ch, *ch 1, Y-st in next sc, ch 1, sc in next tr; repeat from * to last sc, ch 1, (Y-st, ch 1, tr) in last sc, turn.

Row 4: Ch 7, sc in 2nd ch from hook, ch 1, skip next 2 ch, shell in next ch, ch 1, skip next 2 ch, sc in next tr, *ch 1, skip next ch-1 space, shell in next ch-1 space, ch 1, sc in next sc; repeat from * to last 3 sc, ch 1, skip next 2 sc, (shell, ch 1, tr) in last sc, turn. (18 (19, 21, 22, 23, 25, 26) shells)

Row 5: Ch 11, sc in 2nd ch from hook and in next 6 ch, ch 1, Y-st in next tr, *ch 1, sc in next tr, ch 1, Y-st in next sc; repeat from * to last sc, ch 1, (Y-st, ch 1, tr) in last sc, turn.

Row 6: Ch 7, sc in 2nd ch from hook, ch 1, skip next 2 ch, shell in next ch, ch 1, skip next 2 ch, sc in next tr, *ch 1, skip next ch-1 space, shell in next ch-1 space, ch 1, sc in next sc; repeat from * to last 6 sc, ch 1, skip next 2 sc, shell in next sc, ch 1, skip next 2 sc, sc in last sc, turn. (21 (22, 24, 25, 26, 28, 29) shells)

Row 7: Repeat Row 3.

Row 8: Ch 8, shell in 6th ch from hook, ch 1, sc in next tr, *ch 1, skip next ch-1 space, shell in next ch-1 space, ch 1, sc in next sc; repeat from * to last 3 sc, ch 1, skip next 2 sc, (shell, ch 1, tr) in last sc, turn. (24 (25, 27, 28, 29, 31, 32) shells)

Row 9: Ch 8, sc in 2nd ch from hook and in next 3 ch, ch 1, Y-st in next tr, ch 1, sc in next tr, *ch 1, Y-st in next sc, ch 1, sc in next tr; repeat from * to turning ch, ch 1, (Y-st, ch 1, tr) in 4th ch of turning ch, turn.

Row 10: Repeat Row 8. (27 (28, 30, 31, 32, 34, 35) shells)

Row 11: Ch 5, dc in 5th ch from hook, ch 1, skip first tr, sc in next tr, *ch 1, Y-st in next sc, ch 1, sc in next tr; repeat from * to turning ch, ch 1, tr in 4th ch of turning ch, dc in base of tr just made, turn.

Row 12: Ch 4 (counts as dc, ch 1), (tr, ch 1, dc) in first dc (first shell made), ch 1, sc in next sc, *ch 1, skip next ch-1 space, shell in next ch-1 space, ch 1, sc in next sc; repeat from * to turning ch, ch 1, shell in top of turning ch, turn. (28 (29, 31, 32, 33, 35, 36) shells)

Row 13: Ch 5, dc in 5th ch from hook, ch 1, sc in next tr, *ch 1, Y-st in next sc, ch 1, sc in next tr; repeat from * to turning ch, ch 1, tr in 3rd ch of turning ch, dc in base of tr just made, turn.

Row 14: Ch 5, dc in first dc, ch 1, sc in next sc, *ch 1, skip next ch-1 space, shell in next ch-1 space, ch 1, sc in next sc; repeat from * to last ch-1 space, ch 1, skip last ch-1 space, (dc, ch 1, tr) in top of turning ch, turn. (27 (28, 30, 31, 32, 34, 35) shells)

Row 15: Ch 1, sc in first tr, *ch 1, Y-st in next sc, ch 1, sc in next tr; repeat from * across working last sc in 4th ch of turning ch, turn.

Row 16: Ch 1, sc in first sc, *ch 1, skip next ch-1 space, shell in next ch-1 space, ch 1, sc in next sc; repeat from * across, turn. (28 (29, 31, 32, 33, 35, 36) shells)

Row 17: Ch 5, dc in 5th ch from hook, *ch 1, sc in next tr, ch 1, Y-st in next sc; repeat from * to last sc, tr in last sc, dc in base of tr just made, turn.

Rows 18–23: Repeat rows 12–17.

Sizes L (1X, 2X, 3X) only

Rows 24–25 (25, 27, 27): Repeat rows 12–13 (13, 15, 15).

All Sizes: Fasten off

Right Front

With 2 strands of thread held together, ch 47 (47, 53, 53, 59, 65, 71).

Row 1 (right side): Sc in 2nd ch from hook, *ch 1, skip next 2 ch, shell in next ch, ch 1, skip next 2 ch, sc in next ch; repeat from * to last 3 ch, ch 1, skip next 2 ch, (dc, ch 1, tr) in last ch, turn. (7 (7, 8, 8, 9, 10, 11) shells)

Row 2: Ch 1, sc in first tr, *ch 1, Y-st in next sc, ch 1, sc in next tr; repeat from * to last sc, ch 1, dc in last sc, turn.

Row 3: Ch 4, sc in next sc, *ch 1, skip next ch-1 space, shell in next ch-1 space, ch 1, sc in next sc; repeat from * across, turn.

Row 4: Ch 4 (counts as tr), dc in 4th ch from hook, ch 1, sc in next tr, *ch 1, Y-st in next sc, ch 1, sc in next tr; repeat from * to last sc, ch 1, Y-st in last sc, dc in 3rd ch of turning ch, turn.

Row 5: Ch 1, shell in first ch-1 space, ch 1, sc in next sc, *ch 1, skip next ch-1 space, shell in next ch-1 space, ch 1, sc in next sc; repeat from * to last ch-1 space, ch 1, skip last ch-1 space, (dc, ch 1, tr) in top of turning ch, turn.

Row 6: Ch 1, sc in first tr, *ch 1, Y-st in next sc, ch 1, sc in next tr; repeat from * across, turn; leave remaining sts unworked, turn.

Row 7: Ch 1, sc in first sc, *ch 1, skip next ch-1 space, shell in next ch-1 space, ch 1, sc in next sc; repeat from * across, turn.

Row 8: Ch 4, dc in 4th ch from hook, ch 1, sc in next tr, *ch 1, Y-st in next sc, ch 1, sc in next tr; repeat from * to last sc, ch 1, tr in last sc, dc in base of tr just made, turn.

Row 9: Ch 5, dc in first dc, ch 1, sc in next sc, *ch 1, skip next ch-1 space, shell in next ch-1 space, ch 1, sc in next sc; repeat from * to turning ch, ch 1, (dc, ch 1, tr) in top of turning ch, turn.

Sizes L (1X, 2X, 3X) only

Rows 10 to 13 (13, 17, 17): Repeat last 4 rows 1 (1, 2, 2) more times.

Note: When repeating row 6, there will be no stitches to leave unworked at the end of the row. Work all the way across working last sc in 4th ch of turning ch.

Shape sleeve

Row 1 (wrong side): Ch 7, sc in 2nd ch from hook and place marker in sc just made (for seaming), sc in next 5 ch, sc in next tr, *ch 1, Y-st in next sc, ch 1, sc in next tr; repeat from * across working last sc in 4th ch of turning ch, turn.

Row 2: Ch 1, skip first ch-1 space, shell in next ch-1 space, ch 1, sc in next sc, *ch 1, skip next ch-1 space, shell in next ch-1 space, ch 1, sc in next sc; repeat from * to last 6 sc, ch 1, skip next 2 sc, shell in next sc, ch 1, skip next 2 sc, sc in last sc, turn. (8 (8, 9, 10, 11, 12, 13) shells)

Row 3: Ch 8, sc in 2nd ch from hook and in next 3 ch, *ch 1, Y-st in next sc, ch 1, sc in next tr; repeat from * across working last sc in last tr, turn; leave remaining sts unworked.

Row 4: Ch 1, sc in first sc, *ch 1, skip next ch-1 space, shell in next ch-1 space, ch 1, sc in next sc; repeat from * to last 3 sc, ch 1, skip next 2 sc, (shell, ch 1, tr) in last sc, turn. (9 (9, 10, 11, 12, 13, 14) shells)

Row 5: Ch 11, sc in 2nd ch from hook and in next 6 ch, ch 1, sc in next tr, *ch 1, Y-st in next sc, ch 1, sc in next tr; repeat from * to last sc, ch 1, tr in last sc, dc in base of tr just made, turn.

Row 6: Ch 5, dc in first dc, ch 1, sc in next sc, *ch 1, skip next ch-1 space, shell in next ch-1 space, ch 1, sc in next sc; repeat from * to last 6 sc, ch 1, skip next 2 sc, shell in next sc, ch 1, skip next 2 sc, sc in last sc, turn. (10 (10, 11, 12, 13, 14, 15) shells)

Row 7: Ch 8, sc in 2nd ch from hook and in next 3 ch, *ch 1, Y-st in next sc, ch 1, sc in next tr; repeat from * across working last sc in 4th ch of turning ch, turn.

Row 8: *Ch 1, skip next ch-1 space, shell in next ch-1 space, ch 1, sc in next sc; repeat from * to last 3 sc, ch 1, skip next 2 sc, (shell, ch 1, tr) in last sc, turn. (12 (12, 13, 14, 15, 16, 17) shells)

Rows 9 and 10: Repeat rows 3 and 4. (13 (13, 14, 15, 16, 17, 18) shells)

Row 11: Ch 5, dc in 5th ch from hook, ch 1, skip first tr, sc in next tr, *ch 1, Y-st in next sc, ch 1, sc in next tr; repeat from * to last sc, ch 1, tr in last sc, dc in base of tr just made, turn.

Row 12: Ch 5, dc in first dc, ch 1, sc in next sc, *ch 1, skip next ch-1 space, shell in next ch-1 space, ch 1, sc in next sc; repeat from * to turning ch, ch 1, shell in top of turning ch, turn.

Row 13: Ch 5, dc in 5th ch from hook, ch 1, sc in next tr, ch 1, Y-st in next sc, *ch 1, sc in next tr, ch 1, Y-st in next sc; repeat from * to turning ch, ch 1, sc in 4th ch of turning ch, turn.

Row 14: Ch 1, sc in first sc, *ch 1, skip next ch-1 space, shell in next ch-1 space, ch 1, sc in next sc; repeat from * to last ch-1 space, ch 1, skip last ch-1 space, (dc, ch 1, tr) in top of turning ch, turn.

Row 15: Ch 1, sc in first tr, *ch 1, Y-st in next sc, ch 1, sc in next tr; repeat from * to last sc, tr in last sc, turn.

Row 16: Ch 1, skip first tr, sc in next sc, *ch 1, skip next ch-1 space, shell in next ch-1 space, ch 1, sc in next sc; repeat from * across, turn.

Row 17: Ch 5, dc in 5th ch from hook, *ch 1, sc in next tr, ch 1, Y-st in next sc; repeat from * to last sc, tr in last sc, dc in base of tr just made, turn.

Rows 18–23: Repeat rows 12–17.

Sizes L (1X, 2X, 3X) only

Rows 24–25 (25, 27, 27): Repeat rows 12–13 (13, 15, 15).

All Sizes: Fasten off.

Left front

Start: With 2 strands of thread held together, ch 47 (47, 53, 53, 59, 65, 71).

Row 1 (right side): Dc in 5th ch from hook, ch 1, skip next 2 ch, sc in next ch, *ch 1, skip next 2 ch, shell in next ch, ch 1, skip next 2 ch, sc in next ch; repeat from * to last 3 ch, ch 1, skip next 2 ch, (dc, ch 1, tr) in last ch, turn—7 (7, 8, 8, 9, 10, 11) shells)

Row 2: Ch 4, sc in first tr, *ch 1, Y-st in next sc, ch 1, sc in next tr; repeat from * across working last sc in 4th ch of turning ch, turn.

Row 3: Ch 1, sc in first sc, *ch 1, skip next ch-1 space, shell in next ch-1 space, ch 1, sc in next sc; repeat from * to turning ch, ch 1, dc in 2nd ch of turning ch, turn. (8 (8, 9, 9, 10, 11, 12) shells)

Row 4: *Ch 1, Y-st in next sc, ch 1, sc in next tr; repeat from * to last sc, ch 1, tr in last sc, dc in base of tr just made, turn.

Row 5: Ch 5, dc in first dc, ch 1, sc in next sc, *ch 1, skip next ch-1 space, shell in next ch-1 space, ch 1, sc in next sc; repeat from * to last Y-st, ch 1, dc in ch-1 space of last Y-st, ch 1, tr-dc-tog over same ch-1 space and next tr, turn. (7 (7, 8, 8, 9, 10, 11) shells)

Row 6: Ch 1, sc in first st, *ch 1, Y-st in next sc, ch 1, sc in next tr; repeat from * across working last sc in 4th ch of turning ch, turn.

Row 7: Ch 1, sc in first sc, *ch 1, skip next ch-1 space, shell in next ch-1 space, ch 1, sc in next sc; repeat from * across, turn. (8 (8, 9, 9, 10, 11, 12) shells)

Row 8: Ch 4, sc in next tr, *ch 1, Y-st in next sc, ch 1, sc in next tr; repeat from * to last sc, ch 1, tr in last sc, dc in base of tr just made, turn.

Row 9: Ch 5, dc in first dc, ch 1, sc in next sc, *ch 1, skip next ch-1 space, shell in next ch-1 space, ch 1, sc in next sc; repeat from * to turning ch, ch 1, dc in top of turning ch, turn. (7 (7, 8, 8, 9, 10, 11) shells)

Sizes L (1X, 2X, 3X) only

Rows 10 to 13 (13, 17, 17): Repeat last 4 rows 1 (1, 2, 2) more times.

Shape sleeve

Row 1: *Ch 1, Y-st in next sc, ch 1, sc in next tr; repeat from * across working last sc in 4th ch of turning ch, turn.

Row 2: Ch 7, sc in 2nd ch from hook, place marker in sc just made for seaming, ch 1, skip next 2 ch, shell in next ch, skip next 2 ch, sc in next sc, *ch 1, skip next ch-1 space, shell in next ch-1 space, ch 1, sc in next sc; repeat from * to last Y-st, ch 1, (dc, ch 1, tr) in ch-1 space of last Y-st, turn. (8 (8, 9, 9, 10, 11, 12) shells)

Row 3: Ch 1, sc in first tr, *ch 1, Y-st in next sc, ch 1, sc in next tr; repeat from * to last sc, ch 1, (Y-st, ch 1, tr) in last sc, turn.

Row 4: Ch 7, sc in 2nd ch from hook, ch 1, skip next 2 ch, shell in next ch, ch 1, skip next 2 ch, sc in next tr, *ch 1, skip next ch-1 space, shell in next ch-1 space, ch 1, sc in next sc; repeat from * across, turn. (10 (10, 11, 11, 12, 13, 14) shells)

Row 5: Ch 4, sc in next tr, *ch 1, Y-st in next sc, ch 1, sc in next tr; repeat from * to last sc, ch 1, (Y-st, ch 1, tr) in last sc, turn.

Row 6: Ch 7, sc in 2nd ch from hook, ch 1, skip next 2 ch, shell in next ch, ch 1, skip next 2 ch, sc in next tr, *ch 1, skip next ch-1 space, shell in next ch-1 space, ch 1, sc in next sc; repeat from * to turning ch, ch 1, dc in 3rd ch of turning ch, turn. (11 (11, 12, 12, 13, 14, 15) shells)

Row 7: *Ch 1, Y-st in next sc, ch 1, sc in next tr; repeat from * to last sc, ch 1, (Y-st, ch 1, tr) in last sc, turn.

Row 8: Ch 8, shell in 6th ch from hook, ch 1, skip next 2 ch, sc in next tr, *ch 1, skip next ch-1 space, shell in next ch-1 space, ch 1, sc in next sc; repeat from * to last Y-st, ch 1, dc in ch-1 space of last Y-st, ch 1, tr-dc-tog over same ch-1 space and last tr, turn. (12 (12, 13, 13, 14, 15, 16) shells)

Row 9: Ch 1, sc in first st, *ch 1, Y-st in next sc, ch 1, sc in next tr; repeat from * to turning ch, ch 1, skip next ch, (Y-st, ch 1, tr) in 4th ch of turning ch, turn.

Row 10: Ch 8, shell in 6th ch from hook, ch 1, skip next 2 ch, sc in next tr, *ch 1, skip next ch-1 space, shell in next ch-1 space, ch 1, sc in next sc; repeat from * across, turn. (14 (14, 15, 15, 16, 17, 18) shells)

Row 11: Ch 4, sc in next tr, *ch 1, Y-st in next sc, ch 1, sc in next tr; repeat from * to turning ch, ch 1, tr in 4th ch of turning ch, dc in base of tr just made, turn.

Row 12: Ch 4, shell in first dc, ch 1, sc in next sc, *ch 1, skip next ch-1 space, shell in next ch-1 space, ch 1, sc in next sc; repeat from * to turning ch, ch 1, dc in 3rd ch of turning ch, turn.

Row 13: *Ch 1, Y-st in next sc, ch 1, sc in next tr; repeat from * to turning ch, ch 1, tr in 3rd ch of turning ch, dc in base of tr just made, turn.

Row 14: Ch 5, dc in first dc, ch 1, sc in next sc, *ch 1, skip next ch-1 space, shell in next ch-1 space, ch 1, sc in next sc; repeat from * to last Y-st, ch 1, (dc, ch 1, tr) in ch-1 space of last Y-st, turn. (13 (13, 14, 14, 15, 16, 17) shells)

Row 15: Ch 1, sc in first tr, ch 1, Y-st in next sc, *ch 1, sc in next tr, ch 1, Y-st in next sc; repeat from * to turning ch, ch 1, sc in 4th ch of turning ch, turn.

Row 16: Ch 1, sc in first sc, *ch 1, skip next ch-1 space, shell in next ch-1 space, ch 1, sc in next sc; repeat from * across, turn. (14 (14, 15, 15, 16, 17, 18) shells)

Row 17: Ch 4, sc in next tr, *ch 1, Y-st in next sc, ch 1, sc in next tr; repeat from * to last sc, ch 1, tr in last sc, dc in base of tr just made, turn.

Rows 18 to 23: Repeat rows 12–17.

Sizes L (1X, 2X, 3X) only

Rows 24–25 (25, 27, 27): Repeat rows 12–13 (13, 15, 15).

All sizes: Fasten off.

Finishing

Wet block the pieces for the best results. With the right sides together, align the underarm markers and sew the side and underarm seams together. Remove the markers.

Front edging

Work edging with 2 strands of thread held together.

Row 1 (right side): With right side facing, join thread in lower front corner to work up a front edge, work sc evenly spaced up the front edge, across back neck, and down other front edge, turn, do not continue across lower edge.

Rows 2 to 4: Ch 1, sc in each st across, turn.

Row 5: Skip first sc, slip st in each sc across.

Fasten off.

Lower edging and tie

Work edging and ties with 2 strands of thread held together.

Row 1 (right side): Ch 36 for first tie, with right side facing, slip st to lower front corner to work across the lower edge, sc evenly spaced across lower edge, ch 37 for 2nd tie, turn.

Row 2: Sc in 2nd ch from hook and in each ch across tie ch, sc in each sc across to other tie ch, sc in each ch across, turn.

Rows 3 and 4: Ch 1, sc in each st across, turn.

Row 5: Skip first sc, slip st in each sc across.

Fasten off.

Weave in ends.

Do wet block edging if desired.

12. A Shawl in Contrasting Stripes for Colder Weather

The stitches this shawl is made to produce a tightly-structured fabric that is perfect for colder days. It has alternating stripes in a main and a contrasting color (Fedotova, 2018).

Supplies needed:

- 1 skein of super fine yarn in the main color
- 2 skeins of super fine yarn in the contrasting color
- Crochet hook, E-4 (3.5 mm)
- A tapestry needle
- Stitch marker

Abbreviations:

- ch = chain
- st/s = stitch/es
- dc = double crochet
- cc = contrasting color
- patt = pattern
- rep = repeat
- sc = single crochet
- sk = skip
- FPdc = front post double crochet
- FPdc2tog = two front post double crochet together
- M = marker
- MC = main color
- PM = place marker

Gauge: 20 stitches and 15 rows = 4 inches in textured stitch pattern.

Specifics:

The finished measurements are a length of 55¼ inches and a width of 22½ inches.

The shawl is worked in back loops, front post stitches, single crochet, and double crochet.

To prevent tightening of the fabric, work all FP stitches higher than usual—crochet them right under the tops instead of around the posts. You can also work the last st of each row higher (hdc and tr instead of sc and dc) to help prevent tightening along the top of the shawl.

Pattern:

Start: The work is started with a magic ring.

Row 1 (right side): With MC, 5 sc in magic ring. Turn. (5 sts)

Row 2 (wrong side): Ch 3 (counts as dc here and throughout), 2 dc in first st, 1 dc in next st, 5 dc in next st, PM in center (third) st, 1 dc in next st, 3 dc in last st. Turn. (13 sts). Move M up to center st each row.

Row 3: Ch 1, 2 sc in first st, 1 sc in next st, FPdc around first sc two rows below, sk 1 dc, 1 sc in next st, FPdc around next (second) sc two rows below, sk 1 dc, 1 sc in next st, FPdc around same (second) sc two rows below, 1 sc in marked st, FPdc around next (third) sc two rows below, 1 sc in next st, FPdc around same (third) sc two rows below, sk 1 dc, 1 sc in next st, FPdc around next (fourth) sc two rows below, sk 1 dc, 1 sc in next st, 2 sc in last st. Turn. (17 sts)

Row 4: Ch 3, 2 dc in first st, dc across to M, 5 dc in marked st, dc across to last st, 3 dc in last st. Turn. (25 sts)

Row 5: Ch 1, 2 sc in first st, FPdc around first sc two rows below, sk 1 dc, 1 sc in next st, FPdc around next (second) sc two rows below, sk 1 dc, 1 sc in next st, [FPdc around next FPdc, sk 1 dc, 1 sc in next st] across to one st before M, FPdc around previously used FPdc, sk 1 dc, 3 sc in marked st, FPdc around next FPdc, sk 1 dc, 1 sc in next st, FPdc around previously used FPdc, sk 1 dc, 1 sc in next st, [FPdc around next FPdc, sk 1 dc, 1 sc in next st] across to last four sts, [FPdc around next sc two rows below, sk 1 dc, 1 sc in next st] twice, 1 sc in last (just used) st. Turn. (29 sts)

Row 6: As Row 4. (37 sts)

Row 7: Ch 1, 2 sc in first st, 1 sc in next st, FPdc around first sc two rows below, sk 1 dc, 1 sc in next st, [FPdc around next FPdc, sk 1 dc, 1 sc in next st] across to two sts before M, FPdc around next sc two rows below, sk 1 dc, 1 sc in next st, FPdc around previously used sc two rows below, 1 sc in marked st, FPdc around next sc two rows below, 1 sc in next st, FPdc around previously used sc two rows below, sk 1 dc, 1 sc in next st, [FPdc around next FPdc, sk 1 dc, 1 sc in next st] across to last three sts, FPdc around next sc two rows below (2nd to last sc), sk 1 dc, 1 sc in next st, 2 sc in last st. Turn. Cut yarn. (41 sts)

Ribbing stitch pattern

Row 8: With CC and working in back loop only, ch 1, 2 sc in first st, sc across to M, 3 sc in marked st, sc across to last st, working in both loops, 2 sc in last st. Turn. (45 sts)

Rows 9 to 11: As row 8. (57 sts)

Diamond stitch pattern

Row 12: Continue with CC, ch 3, 2 dc in first st, dc across to M, 3 dc in marked st, dc across to last st, 3 dc in last st. Turn. (63 sts)

Row 13: Ch 1, 1 sc in first st, FPdc around first sc two rows below, 3 sc, [FPdc2tog around previously used sc and next fourth sc two rows below, sk 1 dc, 3 sc] across to M (last sc is worked in marked st), FPdc around previously used sc, 1 sc in same (marked) st, 2 sc, [FPdc2tog around previously used sc and next fourth sc two rows below, sk 1 dc, 3 sc] across to last five sts,

FPdc2tog around previously used st and next third sc two rows below (2nd to last sc), sk 1 dc, 3 sc, FPdc around previously used sc, 1 sc in last st. Turn. (67 sts)

Row 14: As row 12. (73 sts)

Row 15: Ch 1, 2 sc in first st, 4 sc, FPdc2tog around FPdc and next FPdc2tog, sk 1 dc, 3 sc, [FPdc2tog around previously used and next FPdc2tog, sk 1 dc, 3 sc] across to three sts before M, FPdc2tog around previously used FPdc2tog and next FPdc, sk 1 dc, 2 sc, 3 sc in marked st, 2 sc, FPdc2tog around previously used FPdc and next FPdc2tog, sk 1 dc, 3 sc, [FPdc2tog around previously used and next FPdc2tog, sk 1 dc, 3 sc] across to last six sts, FPdc2tog around previously used FPdc2tog and last FPdc, sk 1 dc, 4 sc, 2 sc in last st. Turn. (77 sts)

Ribbing stitch pattern

Rows 16 to 19: As row 8. Cut yarn. (93 sts)

Textured stitch pattern

Row 20: With MC, as Row 4. (101 sts)

Row 21: Ch 1, 2 sc in first st, 1 sc in next st, FPdc around first sc two rows below, sk 1 dc, 1 sc in next st, [sk 1 sc two rows below, FPdc around next sc, sk 1 dc, 1 sc in next st] across to two sts before M, FPdc around next sc two rows below, sk 1 dc, 1 sc in next st, FPdc around previously used sc, 1 sc in marked st, FPdc around next sc two rows below, 1 sc in next st, FPdc around previously used sc, sk 1 dc, 1 sc in next st, [sk 1 sc two rows below, FPdc around next sc, sk 1 dc, 1 sc in next st] across to last three sts, FPdc around next sc two rows below (2nd to last sc), sk 1 dc, 1 sc in next st, 2 sc in last st. Turn. (105 sts)

Row 22: As row 4. (113 sts)

Row 23: As row 5. (117 sts)

Row 24: As row 4. 125 sts

Row 25: As row 7. Cut yarn. (129 sts)

Repeat rows 8 to 25 twice, repeat rows 8 to 19 once.

Fasten off and weave in ends.

13. Wrap Yourself in Lattice Lace

A soft, lacy, yet warm wrap in two colors (Caron, n.d.).

Supplies needed:

- 4 skeins of very soft Aran yarn, more than 3-ply, in the main color
- 1 skein of very soft Aran yarn, more than 3-ply, in the contrasting color
- Crochet hook, J-10 (6mm)
- A yarn sewing needle

Abbreviations:

- ch = chain
- st/s = stitch/es
- dc = double crochet
- CC = contrasting color
- sc = single crochet
- tr = treble crochet
- MC = main color
- sl st = slip stitch

Gauge: In single crochet, 10 stitches and 12 rows = 4 inches.

Specifics:

The finished measurements are approximately 24 inches wide by 65 inches long. If you want the wrap to be narrower, chain 62 to begin. That will create a wrap about 20 inches wide.

Crochet the chains for the foundation loosely or use a larger hook (US size K-10.5 (6.5 mm)) to work it.

Pattern:

Start: With MC, ch 74.

Row 1: Sc in second ch from hook and next 3 ch, ch 7, skip next 5 ch, *sc in next 7 ch, ch 7, skip next 5 ch;

repeat from * to last 4 ch, sc in last 4 ch, turn. (6 ch-7 sp)

Row 2: Ch 1, sc in first 3 sc, ch 5, skip next sc, skip next 3 ch, sc in next ch (center ch of ch-7 sp), ch 5, skip next 3 ch, skip next sc, *sc in next 5 sc, ch 5, skip next sc, skip next 3 ch, sc in next ch, ch 5, skip next 3 ch, skip next sc; repeat from * across to last 3 sc, sc in last 3 sc, turn. (12 ch-5 sp)

Row 3: Ch 1, sc in first 2 sc, ch 5, skip next sc, skip next 4 ch, sc in next ch, sc in next sc, sc in next ch, ch 5, skip next 4 ch, skip next sc, *sc in next 3 sc, ch 5, skip next sc, skip next 4 ch, sc in next ch, sc in next sc, sc in next ch, ch 5, skip next 4 ch, skip next sc; repeat from * across to last 2 sc, sc in last 2 sc, turn.

Row 4: Ch 1, sc in first sc, ch 5, skip next sc, skip next 4 ch, sc in next ch, sc in next 3 sc, sc in next ch, ch 5, skip next 4 ch, skip next sc, *sc in next sc, ch 5, skip next sc, skip next 4 ch, sc in next ch, sc in next 3 sc, sc in next ch, ch 5, skip next 4 ch, skip next sc; repeat from * across to last sc, sc in last sc, turn.

Row 5: Ch 7 (counts as tr, ch 3), skip first sc, skip next 4 ch, sc in next ch, sc in next 5 sc, sc in next ch, *ch 7, skip next 4 ch, skip next sc, skip next 4 ch, sc in next ch, sc in next 5 sc, sc in next ch; repeat from * across to last chsp, ch 3, skip last 4 ch, tr in last sc, turn.

Row 6: Ch 1, sc in first tr, ch 5, skip first ch-3 sp, skip next sc, sc in next 5 sc, ch 5, skip next sc, *skip next 3 ch, sc in next ch (center ch of ch-7 sp), ch 5, skip next 3 ch, skip next sc, sc in next 5 sc, ch 5, skip next sc; repeat from * across to last ch-sp, sc in 4th ch of beginning ch-7, turn.

Row 7: Ch 1, sc in first sc, sc in next ch, ch 5, skip next 4 ch, skip next sc, sc in next 3 sc, ch 5, skip next sc, *skip next 4 ch, sc in next ch, sc in next sc, sc in next ch, ch 5, skip next 4 ch, skip next sc, sc in next 3 sc, ch 5, skip next sc; repeat from * across to last ch-sp, skip last 4 ch, sc in next ch, sc in last sc, turn.

Row 8: Ch 1, sc in first 2 sc, sc in next ch, ch 5, skip next 4 ch, skip next sc, sc in next sc, ch 5, skip next sc, skip next 4 ch, sc in next ch, *sc in next 3 sc, sc in next ch, ch 5, skip next 4 ch, skip next sc, sc in next sc, ch 5, skip next sc, skip next 4 ch, sc in next ch; repeat from * across to last 2 sc, sc in last 2 sc, turn.

Row 9: Ch 1, sc in first 3 sc, sc in next ch, ch 7, skip next 4 ch, skip next sc, skip next 4 ch, sc in next ch, *sc in next 5 sc, sc in next ch, ch 7, skip next 4 ch, skip next sc, skip next 4 ch, sc in next ch; repeat from * across to last 3 sc, sc in last 3 sc, turn. Repeat Rows 2–9 until piece measures 65"/165 cm, or desired length, end by working a row 5. Do not fasten off.

Finishing

Round 1: Pivot to work in ends of rows along long side, work 2 sc around each tr or ch-3 sp and 1 sc around each sc along side; pivot to work in the free loops on the opposite side of the foundation chain, sc in the base of each sc, 6 sc in each ch-5 sp across foundation ch; pivot to work in ends of rows along the opposite long side of piece, work 2 sc around each tr or ch-3 sp and 1 sc around each sc along side; pivot to work in the sts of the last row of wrap, 3 sc in first and last ch-3 sp, sc in each sc, 6 sc in each ch-7 sp across row; join with slip st in first sc.

Fasten off.

Round 2 (picot round): Join CC anywhere in edge, *(sc, ch 3, slip st in 3rd ch from hook, sc) in next sc, skip next sc; repeat from * around edge; join with slip st in first sc.

Fasten off and weave in all ends.

Lay piece flat and wet-block if desired.

14. Amigurumi Octopus

Delight a little one with a friendly stuffed octopus (Delaney, 2019).

Supplies needed:

- 1 skein of DK yarn in the color for the body (A)
- 1 skein of DK yarn in the color for the base, if you want to use a different color (B)
- Enough black yarn to embroider the smile
- Crochet hook, G-6 (4 mm)
- A yarn sewing needle
- Stitch marker
- Fiberfill stuffing

Abbreviations:

- ch = chain
- st/s = stitch/es
- sc = single crochet
- sc2tog = [Insert hook in front loop only of next st] twice; yo and draw loop through both sts, yo and draw through both loops on hook.

Gauge: 20 sc = 4 inches; 16 rounds = 4 inches.

Specifics:

The finished octopus is 6½ inches tall.

Do not join the rounds. Place a stitch marker in the first stitch of the round and move the marker up as the work progresses.

Pattern:

Base

Start: With B, make a loop as if starting with a slip knot and leave a 4-inch tail. Draw the working yarn through the loop and ch 1.

Round 1: 6 sc in ring. Tighten ring.

Round 2: 2 sc in each st around. (12 sts)

Round 3: * Sc in next st, 2 sc in next st; repeat from * around. (18 sts)

Round 4: * Sc in next 2 sts, 2 sc in next st; repeat from * around. (24 sts)

Round 5: * Sc in next 2 sts, 2 sc in next st; repeat from * around. (32 sts.)

Round 6: * Sc in next 3 sts, 2 sc in next st; repeat from * around. (40 sts)

Round 7: * Sc in next st, dc in next 3 sts, sc in next st; repeat from * around.

Round 8: * Sc in next 2 sts, dc in next st, sc in next 2 sts; repeat from * around.

Fasten off and weave in the ends.

Head and body

Start to round 3: With A, work same as base through round 3.

Round 4: Sc in each st around.

Round 5: * Sc in next 2 sts, 2 sc in next st; repeat from * around. (24 sts)

Round 6: Repeat round 4.

Round 7: * Sc in next 3 sts, 2 sc in next st; repeat from * around – 30 sts)

Round 8: * Sc in next 4 sts, 2 sc in next st; repeat from * around. (36 sts)

Rounds 9 to 14: Repeat round 4.

Begin Short Row Shaping-Row 15: Sc in next 32 sts, slip st in next st; turn.

Row 16: Skip first sc, sc in next 30 sts, slip st in next st; turn.

Row 17: Skip first sc, sc in next 28 sts, slip st in next st; turn.

Row 18: Skip first sc, sc in next 26 sts, slip st in next st; turn.

Row 19: Skip first sc, sc in next 24 sts, slip st in next st; turn.

Row 20: Skip first sc, sc in next 22 sts, slip st in next st; turn.

End Short Row Shaping-Round 21: Ch 1, sc in each st around. (36 sts)

Round 22: * Sc in next 4 sts, sc2tog; repeat from * around. (30 sts)

Round 23: * Sc in next 3 sts, sc2tog; repeat from * around. (24 sts)

Round 24: * Sc in next 2 sts, sc2tog; repeat from * around. (18 sts.)

Rounds 25 & 26: Sc in each st around.

Round 27: * Sc in next 2 sts, 2 sc in next st; repeat from * around. (24 sts)

Round 28: * Sc in next 2 sts, 2 sc in next st; repeat from * around. (32 sts)

Round 29: * Sc in next st, 2 dc in next st, dc in next st, sc in next st; repeat from * around. (40 sts)

Round 30: * Sc in next 2 sts, dc in next st, sc in next 2 sts; repeat from * around.

Attach eyes to the points made by the short rows and match them. (If the toy is for a small child, rather embroider the eyes for safety).

Round 30 of head & body to round 8 of base. Round 31 will be worked through both layers.

Joining-Round 31: [Sc in next 2 sts, 2 hdc in next st, sc in next 2 sts] 6 times; add stuffing; work directions in brackets 2 more times. (48 sts)

Tentacles-Round 32: * Sc in next 3 sts, ch 32, 2 dc in 3rd ch from hook, [2 dc in next ch] 29 times; sc in next 3 sts; repeat from * around. (8 tentacles)

Fasten off and weave in all ends.

Finishing

With C, embroider a smile and weave in all the ends.

15. Poinsettias for the Holidays

A couple of these striking poinsettias scattered on your holiday table will make your decor pop for sure (Gilbank, 2007).

Supplies needed:

- 1 skein each of worsted weight yarn in green, red, and yellow
- Crochet hook, E-4 (3.5 mm)
- A yarn sewing needle
- Stitch marker

Abbreviations:

- ch = chain
- st/s = stitch/es

- sc = single crochet
- sl st = slip stitch
- sc2tog = [Insert hook in front loop only of next st] twice; yo and draw loop through both sts, yo and draw through both loops on hook.

Gauge: Not available.

Specifics:

The finished measurement is a diameter of approximately 5 inches.

Rounds are worked in continuous spirals, do not join them at the ends. Mark the beginning of each round with a stitch marker and move it up with every new round.

You will need six leaves of style A in red, six leaves of style B in green, and one yellow center.

Pattern:

Style A

Start: Make a magic ring, ch 1.

Round 1: 4 sc in magic ring. (4 st)

Round 2: (2 sc in next st, sc in next st) twice. (6 st)

Round 3: (2 sc in next st, sc in next 2 st) twice. (8 st)

Round 4: (2 sc in next st, sc in next 3 st) twice. (10 st)

Round 5: (2 sc in next st, sc in next 4 st) twice. (12 st)

Round 6: (2 sc in next st, sc in next 5 st) twice. (14 st)

Rounds 7 to 8: sc in each st around. (14 st)

Round 9: (invdec, sc in next 5 st) twice. (12 st)

Round 10: (invdec, sc in next 4 st) twice. (10 st)

Round 11: (invdec, sc in next 3 st) twice. (8 st)

Join with sl st to next st.

Fasten off, leaving a long end of yarn.

Style B

Start: Make a magic ring, ch 1.

Round 1: 4 sc in magic ring. (4 st)

Round 2: (2 sc in next st, sc in next st) twice. (6 st)

Round 3: (2 sc in next st, sc in next 2 st) twice. (8 st)

Round 4: (2 sc in next st, sc in next 3 st) twice. (10 st)

Round 5: (2 sc in next st, sc in next 4 st) twice. (12 st)

Round 6: (2 sc in next st, sc in next 5 st) twice. (14 st)

Round 7: (2 sc in next st, sc in next 6 st) twice. (16 st)

Round 8: sc in each st around. (16 st)

Round 9: (invdec, sc in next 6 st) twice. (14 st)

Round 10: (invdec, sc in next 5 st) twice. (12 st)

Round 11: (invdec, sc in next 4 st) twice. (10 st)

Round 12: (invdec, sc in next 3 st) twice. (8 st)

Join with sl st to next st.

Fasten off, leaving a long end of yarn.

Center

Start: Make a magic ring, ch 1.

Round 1: 6 sc in magic ring. (6 st)

Round 2: In front loops only, (sc, ch2, sc) in each st around. (6 loops formed)

Round 3: In remaining back loops of round 1, 5 sc in each st around. (30 st). Allow the stitches of round 3 to crinkle up into a loopy ruffle. They have to stick up to form the center.

Assembly

Step 1: Flatten out each petal.

Style A, step 2: Fold along the centerline, so the two ends of the open edge meet. Keep the edges together with a couple of stitches with a yarn needle and the long yarn end.

String all the petals together on a length of yarn on a yarn needle through the folded edge of each petal. Join them to form a circle, pull the yarn tight and knot it.

Step 2, style B: Arrange one leaf at approximately 60 degrees over a second, so that one side of the open end of one is over the midpoint of the open end of the next like slices of pie.

Stitch them together with small stitches at the end and about a third of the way up the leaves.

Continue until all the leaves are joined and overlapping. There should be a small gap in the center.

Pull any loose ends through to the back.

Final assembly

Arrange the layers by pulling the loose yarn ends through the center hole of the previous layers, so they are all at the back of the flower. The layer order is, bottom to top, B-A-center.

Rotate the layers so all the leaves are visible. Divide the yarn ends at the back into two groups and tie them together in a secure knot.

You can weave in all the yarn ends or leave them long if the poinsettia will be tied onto something.

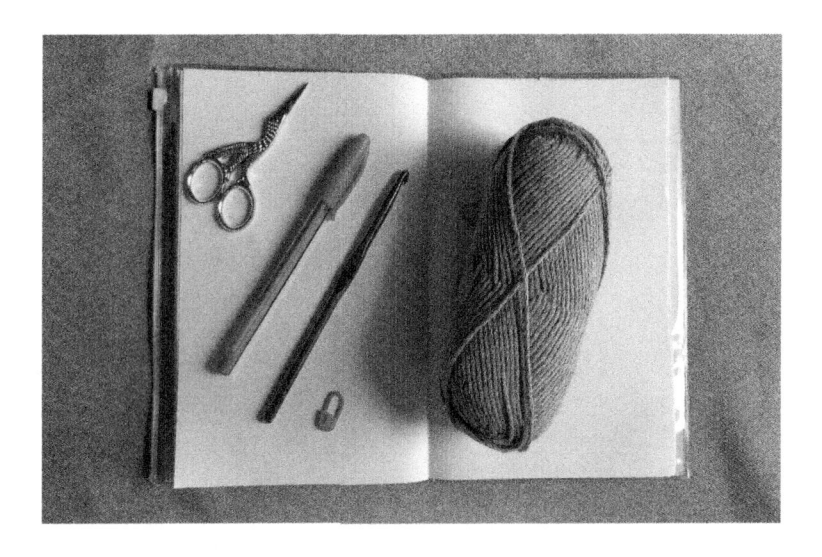

Getting your supplies ready for the next project!

Conclusion

Crocheters are insatiable once the bug has bitten. The patterns in this ebook are not even a drop in the vast ocean of patterns and creations possible with this versatile craft.

Use this ebook as your starting point to keep honing your skills and get inspired to start designing your own patterns.

Review Request

Did you enjoy challenging your skills with the patterns in this ebook? Then please consider leaving a positive review on Amazon, so other crocheters can find it too.

A stylish crocheted doily.

Exclusive 5-day bonus course just for you!

We will be sharing top crafting mistakes to avoid, how to save money on supplies and extra craft patterns!

Simply let us know where to send the course e-mails to via this link below.

https://bit.ly/nancy-gordon

For any general feedback & enquiries, you can reach us at bookgrowthpublishing@mail.com

References

Bittner, M. (2014, July 14). *Celtic weave blanket*. Pattern Paradise. https://pattern-paradise.com/2014/07/14/free-crochet-pattern-celtic-weave-blanket/

Caron. (n.d.). Lattice lace wrap. *Yarnspirations*. https://www.yarnspirations.com/on/demandware.static/-/Sites-master-catalog-spinrite/default/dwa9e5530c/PDF/CAC0126-007292M.pdf

Delaney, S. (2019). *Octopus & Starfish*. Red Heart. https://www.yarnspirations.com/on/demandware.static/-/Sites-master-catalog-spinrite/default/dw2bc25382/PDF/RHC0334-023355M.pdf

Fedotova, E. (2018, January). *Mindfulness*. Www.ravelry.com. https://www.ravelry.com/patterns/sources/m

alabrigo-newsletter-winter-spring-2018/patterns

Gilbank, J. (2007). *Poinsettia*. PlanetJune. https://www.planetjune.com/blog/free-crochet-patterns/poinsettia/

Halsey, A. (2020, December 9). *Tunisian smock stitch cowl pattern*. AllFreeCrochet.com. https://www.allfreecrochet.com/Crocheted-Cowls/Tunisian-Smock-Stitch-Cowl-Pattern

Holloway, K. (2018, November 22). *Granny square pattern: Winter opulence*. Kirsten Holloway Designs. https://kirstenhollowaydesigns.com/2018/11/winter-opulence-crochet-granny-square-pattern.html

Johanson, M. (2020, August 6). *Learn how to crochet a snowflake with this free pattern*. The Spruce Crafts. https://www.thesprucecrafts.com/easy-crochet-snowflake-pattern-979287

Kent, O. (2016, April 22). *Diamond trellis headband*. Hopeful Honey.

http://www.hopefulhoney.com/2016/04/diamond-trellis-headband-free-crochet.html

Pullen, K. (2007). *Broomstick lace capelet.* Crochet Me. https://www.interweave.com/article/crochet/download-six-free-crochet-lace-patterns/

Red Heart. (2021, April 22). *Autumn Butterfly Cardigan.* AllFreeCrochet.com. https://www.allfreecrochet.com/Cardigans-and-Wrap-Sweaters/Autumn-Butterfly-Cardigan-Red-Heart-Yarns

Rubarge, N. (2017). *Bruges Border.* Crochet Me. https://www.interweave.com/article/crochet/download-six-free-crochet-lace-patterns/

Thadani, P. (2015, February 5). *Free pattern for Emily.* Stitches N Scraps. https://stitchesnscraps.com/free-pattern-for-emily/

Toukou, F. (2014). *About Francine Toukou.* Www.francinetoukou.com. https://www.francinetoukou.com/about/

Ventura, C. (1991). *Tapestry crochet heart.* https://www.interweave.com/article/crochet/free-afghan-ebook/

Wilson, M. (2010, April 5). *Cabled wrap.* FaveCrafts.com. https://www.favecrafts.com/Crochet-Clothes-Patterns/Cabled-Wrap-from-Caron-Yarn